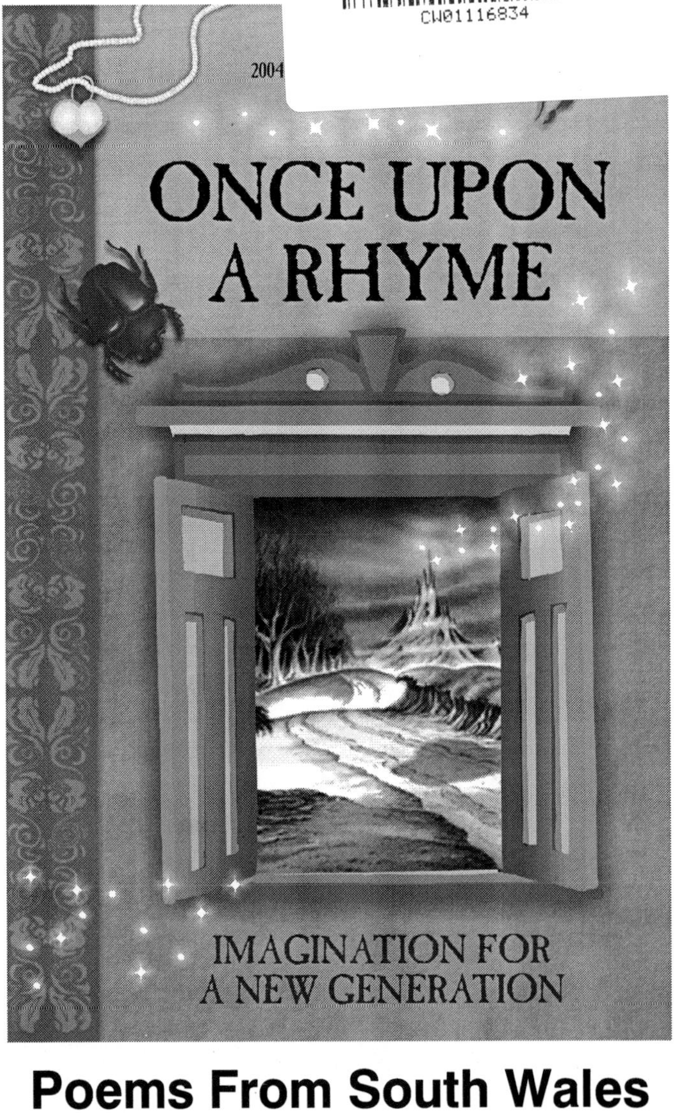
2004
ONCE UPON
A RHYME
IMAGINATION FOR
A NEW GENERATION

Poems From South Wales

Edited by Lynsey Hawkins

First published in Great Britain in 2005 by:
Young Writers
Remus House
Coltsfoot Drive
Peterborough
PE2 9JX
Telephone: 01733 890066
Website: www.youngwriters.co.uk

All Rights Reserved

© *Copyright Contributors 2004*

SB ISBN 1 84460 691 0

Foreword

Young Writers was established in 1991 and has been passionately devoted to the promotion of reading and writing in children and young adults ever since. The quest continues today. Young Writers remains as committed to engendering the fostering of burgeoning poetic and literary talent as ever.

This year's Young Writers competition has proven as vibrant and dynamic as ever and we are delighted to present a showcase of the best poetry from across the UK. Each poem has been carefully selected from a wealth of *Once Upon A Rhyme* entries before ultimately being published in this, our twelfth primary school poetry series.

Once again, we have been supremely impressed by the overall high quality of the entries we have received. The imagination, energy and creativity which has gone into each young writer's entry made choosing the best poems a challenging and often difficult but ultimately hugely rewarding task - the general high standard of the work submitted amply vindicating this opportunity to bring their poetry to a larger appreciative audience.

We sincerely hope you are pleased with our final selection and that you will enjoy *Once Upon A Rhyme Poems From South Wales* for many years to come.

Contents

Coelbren School, Coelbren
Daisy Lea (10)	1
Ffion Powell (10)	1
Cerys Williams (10)	1
Ceinwen Wyke (9)	2
Lloyd Griffiths (9)	2
Bradley Derrick (9)	2
Kimberley Griffiths (9)	3
Emily Jones (9)	3
Danielle Whitney (9)	3
Katy Hodge (8)	4
Ellie Marr (9)	4
Darren Hodge (8)	4
Aled Williams (8)	5
Eva Wallis (7)	5
Rebecca Graham (7)	5
Joe Gorrigan (7)	6

Cwmafan Junior School, Port Talbot
Casey Trott (8)	6
Lois Samuel (8)	7
Ffion James-Hargreaves (8)	7
Lucia Edwards-Collier (9)	8
Jessica Summers (10)	8
Amelia D G Martin (8)	9
Danielle Donovan (8)	9
Rebekah Miles (9)	10
Declan Jones (8)	10
Emily MacDuff (8)	11
Megan Baker (8)	11
Aron Wilkinson (9)	12
Rhianna Hughes (8)	12
Megan Edwards (8)	13
Kayleigh Robins (9)	13
Jordan Heatman (8)	14
Benjamin Rees (9)	14

Gaer Junior School, Newport

Rhian Hillier (10)	15
Lydia Slape (8)	15
Cariad Lewis (9)	16
Curtis Macias (9)	16
Thomas Holtom (10)	17
Adrienne Bartlett (9)	17
Samantha Reardon (10)	18
Bethan Rudd (8)	18
Alex Blackley (10)	19
Jamie Wall (8)	19
Ryan Young (8)	20
Jamie Reed (10)	20
Aimee Hunt (10)	21
Ellis Chapman (8)	21
Ryan Cox (10)	22
Nathan Williams (8)	22
Mark Goddard (10)	23
Abigail Coe (9)	23
Emily Carver (10)	24
Christopher Williams (10)	24
Jade Windsor (10)	25
Matthew Perrin (11)	26
Matthew Thorn (10)	27
James Morgan (11)	28
Sophie Gillard (11)	29
Harriet Oliver (10)	30
Ameen Hail (10)	31
Kieran Farr (11)	32
Scott Mullen (10)	32
Will D Court (10)	33
Lewis Wylie (8)	33
Richard Hills (10)	34
Fedor Tot (10)	35
Charlotte Shadbolt (11)	36
Bethan Maye (10)	37
Sophie Calland (10)	38
James Luckett (8)	38
Joel Kennedy (10)	39
Joshua Wood (8)	39
Amy Turner (10)	40

Aaron Monkley (8) 40
Christopher Powell (10) 41
Kurtis Ormond Crighton (8) 41
Lauren Hillier (10) 42
Hannah Snelling (10) 43
Annalize James (10) 44
Laura Emily Hardwick (10) 45
Ben Williams (10) 46
Sam Gillard (8) 46
Jenna Pullen (10) 47
Sophie Harding (9) 47
Jordan Watkins (10) 48
Cherie Crighton 48
Michael Jones (10) 49
Emily Powell (8) 49
Natalie Luckett (11) 50
Thomas Williams (8) 50
Tom Wilkins (11) 51
Gareth Morgan (8) 51
Ellie Dollery (10) 52
Zaine Said (8) 52
Lincoln Baker (10) 53
Sheldon Campbell-White (8) 53
Lauren Nicola Maggs (10) 54
Ben Ford-Weaver (8) 54
Harry Price (10) 55
Kyle McCarthy (8) 55
Carys Barnett (10) 56

Garnteg Primary School, Pontypool
Danielle Hirons (9) 56
Keelley Quigley (10) 57
Jade Cox (10) 57
Liam Lewis (10) 58
Lauren Harris (9) 58
Jordan White (10) 59
Callum Roynon (9) 59
Holly Parker (9) 60
Kirstie Mayley (10) 60
Tara Earnshaw (9) 60
Jordan Clark (9) 61

Aled Jenkins (10)   61
Kirsty James (9)   61
Derianna Thomas (8)   62
Ieuan Beale (10)   62
Jenna Jones (9)   62
Rachel Gauntlett (8)   63
Lauren Window (8)   63
Thomas Smith (9)   63
Melissa Woollin (8)   64
Bethan George (9)   64
Chloe Harvey-Delahay (9)   64
Emma Frankum (9)   65
Rhys Hatch (8)   65
Ian Powell (9)   65
Bethan Harvey-Delahay (9)   66
Toni Dash (9)   66
Ellis Jones (8)   66

George Street Primary School, Pontypool

Jordan Webb (10)   67
Stephanie Lewis (10)   67
Hannah Haynes (11)   68
Jamie-Leigh Passmore (9)   68
Bethan Jones (10)   69
Lauren Evans (10)   69
Tomos Hewitt (10)   70
Alys Collins (10)   70
Lara Stace (10)   71
Justine Phillips (10)   71
Shane Davis (10)   72
Shona Brandon (10)   72
Samantha Carole Drew (10)   72
Laura Cutter (10)   73
Emma Fellows (10)   73
Adam J Cox (10)   73
Jessica Blanchard (10)   74
Georgia Rice (9)   74
Anna-Marie Bailey (10)   75
Jack Cottrell (10)   75
Emily-Jo Miller (9)   76
Charlotte Taylor (9)   76

Genna Davey (10)	76
Zoë Parker (9)	77
Tansy Lydia Branscombe (9)	77
Samantha Jordan (9)	77
Sian Kinsey (10)	78
Natasha Hirons (9)	78
Megan Jones (9)	79
Callum Griffiths (9)	79
Ross Greasley (9)	79
Sam Haynes (10)	80

Glyncorrwg Primary School, Port Talbot

Jesse Hazeldine (9)	80
Sophie Jones (9)	80
Danielle Down (10)	81
Jasmin Tomlinson (10)	81
Radhika Patel (10)	81
Shannon Spicer (10)	82
Shannon Harris (9)	82
Lowri Radcliffe (10)	82
Kayleigh Protheroe (9)	83
Christopher Howells (10)	83
Thomas Langford (10)	83
Callum Thomas (9)	84
Leigh Baitup (9)	84
Hannah O'Gorman (10)	84
Alissa Bevan (10)	85
Adam Howells (9)	85

Pentrepoeth Junior School, Swansea

Kirsty King (9)	85
Emily Brown (10)	86
Toby Parker (10)	87
Robert Costelloe (9)	87
Melinda Evans (10)	88
Tyler Thomas (8)	88
Luke Gibson (10)	89
Jack Wilcox (8)	89
Jack Penhorwood (10)	90
Alisha Frater-Curtis (10)	90
Caitlin Walters (10)	91

Hannah Gehrke (9)	91
Keiran Miller (10)	92
Natasha Hilde (10)	92
Nathan Young (10)	93
Tyler Ward & Yasmine Grainger (9)	93
Ashley Williams (10)	94
Joshua Bidder (10)	94
Alex Berry (10)	95
Danielle Davies (9)	95
Renée Bull (10)	96
Danielle Williams (10)	97
Scott Piper (11)	98
Sam Matthews (10)	98
Joel Piper (11)	99
Christopher Fisher (10)	100
Karys Turner (8)	100
Amy Raddon (8)	101
Gaby Taylor (8)	101

Pontarddulais Primary School, Swansea

Jake John (10)	101
Greg Cotton (9)	102
Stacey Collier (10)	102
Daniel Jones (10)	102
Steffan Williams (10)	103
James Beynon (10)	103
Jordan Thomas (10)	104
Tom Cowley (10)	104
Lowri Davies (9)	104
Rebecca Aubrey (10)	105
Kurt Thomas (10)	105
Cody-Lea Gross (10)	105
Rebecca Hopkins (9)	106
Michael Grey (9)	106
Tom Hesford (10)	106
Hannah Duncan (10)	107
Liam Chambers (10)	107
Francesca Rix (10)	107
Kayleigh Howells (10)	108
Thomas Evans (10)	108
Charlotte Davies (10)	109

Ashley Mbofana (10)	109
Natasha Harris (10)	109
Louise Eynon (9)	110
Amy Thomas (10)	110
Jodie Rogers (10)	111
James Evans (10)	111
Sam Thomas (10)	112
Jake Thomas (11)	112
Sam Bevan (10)	113
Thomas Lloyd (10)	113
Laura-May James (10)	113
Liam Howells (10)	114
Thomas Brauner (10)	114
Hannah Jones (10)	114
Sophie Burgess (11)	115
Callum Thomas (7)	115
Shaun Harris (7)	115
Reiner Wolf (10)	116
Trystan Bateman (7)	116
Mathew Thomas (7)	116
Myles Oliver Santino Davies (7)	117
Chloe Scott (7)	117
Janine Stephenson (8)	117
Ieuan Derrick (8)	118
Sophie Elizabeth Thomas (7)	118
Sara-Leah Mullen (8)	118
Elinor Eynon (9)	119
Shannon Davies (7)	119
Chloe Rees (7)	119
Chloe Stephenson (10)	120

St Mary's CW Primary School, Brynmawr

Lauran Allford (10)	120
Beth Lewis (10)	121
Laurie Carey (7)	121
Holly Thomas	122
Callum Kershaw	122
Jack James	123
Bethan Jenkins (8)	123
Zoe Pope (10)	124
Molly Tucker (7)	124

Corienne Madden (10)	125
Rhys Cook (7)	125
Nia Follis (9)	126
Hâf Philpotts-Davies (10)	126
Ben Lewis (9)	127
Matthew Lewis-Richards (7)	127
Taylor James (10)	128
Brooke Lewis-Richards (10)	128
Lauren Cook (9)	129
Connor Edwards	129
Gawain Pope (9)	130
Hannah Carey (9)	130
Chloe Jones	131
Elys Philpotts-Davies (10)	131
Della Jenkins (9)	132
Lauren Elias (9)	132
Rebecca Pritchard	133
Danielle Crawford	133
Matthew Collier (9)	134
Adrienne Cox	135
Nina Pickering (9)	135
Regine Tse (9)	136
Meghan Bolter	136
Danielle Cox	137
Lewis Cable	137
Antonia Gullick (8)	138
Jamie Cullinane (10)	138
Salinder Singh	139
Alex Burn (10)	139
Shane Wilcox	139
Morgan Hinton (10)	140
Kieran Puddle	140
Ben Morgan Francis-Adams	140
Katie Prisk (10)	141
Leah Durham (9)	141
Katie Thompson	141
Lauren Parry (9)	142
Taryn Olivia Williams (9)	142
Luke Collier (8)	142
Callum Nuth	143
Alanna Hill (8)	143
Ryan Gardner	143

Paige Stone (8)	144
Liam Davies (8)	144
Louise Bampton	145
Joshua Page (9)	145
Chloe Williams (10)	145

The Poems

Love

Love is white like wedding dresses.
Love feels sweet, happy and joyful.
Love tastes like meringue and wonderful ice cream.
Love smells of tulips and roses.
Love looks romantic.
Love reminds me of weddings.

Daisy Lea (10)
Coelbren School, Coelbren

Fear

Fear is red, like blood.
Fear sounds like people screaming.
Fear feels like a tarantula crawling up your leg.
Fear tastes like your own blood.
Fear smells like everything you're afraid of.
Fear looks like your house is on fire.
Fear reminds me of my first day at school.

Ffion Powell (10)
Coelbren School, Coelbren

Happiness

Happiness is yellow, like the sun.
It feels friendly and good.
It sounds like birds singing.
It tastes like lemon ice cream.
It smells like a roast dinner.
It looks like shining sand.
It reminds me of my friends.

Cerys Williams (10)
Coelbren School, Coelbren

Anger

Anger is red like fire burning in the night.
Anger sounds like a rocket launching.
It feels like heartburn.
It tastes like vindaloo burning inside you.
It looks like the Devil himself.
It reminds me of when I'm bad tempered.

Ceinwen Wyke (9)
Coelbren School, Coelbren

Happiness

Happiness sounds like birds singing.
Happiness tastes like a birthday cake.
Happiness smells of baked brownies.
Happiness looks like a swimming pool.
Happiness feels like a new world.

Lloyd Griffiths (9)
Coelbren School, Coelbren

Fear

Fear is like when you start shivering.
It sounds like someone screaming.
It tastes like ice in your mouth.
It makes you look white.
It smells like a fire that's gone out.
It reminds me of my mother when I show her a frog.

Bradley Derrick (9)
Coelbren School, Coelbren

Happiness

Happiness is multicoloured like a rainbow.
Happiness sounds like a balloon popping.
Happiness feels like you're enjoying yourself.
Happiness tastes like a birthday cake.
Happiness smells like excitement inside you.
Happiness looks like a theme park.
Happiness reminds me of my family.

Kimberley Griffiths (9)
Coelbren School, Coelbren

Love

Love sounds like angels singing.
Love tastes like sweets.
Love smells like flowers.
Love looks like happy babies.
Love feels like soft skin.
Love reminds you of happiness.

Emily Jones (9)
Coelbren School, Coelbren

Hate

Hate is like a devil.
It sounds like a scream.
It feels like a punch.
It smells like gammon.
It tastes like a lemon pancake.
It looks like fire.

Danielle Whitney (9)
Coelbren School, Coelbren

Happiness

Happiness feels like a bubble touched me.
It reminds me of the first time I got a pet.
It smells like the fresh air.
It looks like a fairy coming down from the sky.
It tastes like a rose.
It sounds like children laughing.

Katy Hodge (8)
Coelbren School, Coelbren

Happiness

Happiness is golden, like sandy beaches.
It sounds like a gentle sea.
It tastes sweet like sherbet and strawberries.
It looks pretty and colourful.
It feels good and special.
It reminds me of the best times
And the good things I've done.

Ellie Marr (9)
Coelbren School, Coelbren

Love

Love is pink, like hearts.
It feels pleasant.
It sounds like birds tweeting.
It tastes like cake.
It smells like cherries.
It looks like red berries.
It reminds me of weddings.

Darren Hodge (8)
Coelbren School, Coelbren

Sadness

Sadness is blue, like a whale in its death.
It sounds like a song melting in the sand.
It reminds me of bad times.
It feels like a burn that sticks for hours.
It tastes like a slug that's horrible and green.
It smells like a candle burning to its last.

Aled Williams (8)
Coelbren School, Coelbren

Anger

Anger is like a scarlet fireball.
It sounds like a storm.
It looks like sparks shooting up into the sky.
It feels like a balloon bursting in my hand.
It smells like black smoke.
It tastes like a hot red pepper.
It reminds me of thunder.

Eva Wallis (7)
Coelbren School, Coelbren

Anger

Anger is red like fire.
It sounds like thunder.
It tastes like sour milk.
It smells like smelly socks.
It looks like a bowl of jelly.
It feels like the hot sun.
It reminds me of the Devil.

Rebecca Graham (7)
Coelbren School, Coelbren

Anger

Anger is red like fire.
It looks like blood.
It smells like burnt onions.
It tastes like Devil's breath.
It reminds me of my brother.
It feels like fire shooting up in your body.

Joe Gorrigan (7)
Coelbren School, Coelbren

The Magic Box
(Based on 'Magic Box' by Kit Wright)

I will put in my box . . .
a whole ocean with treasures waiting to be found,
a golden scale from a mystic dragon,
a peg leg from a pirate sailing the seven seas.

I will put in my box . . .
the wisdom of an owl sitting in a silver apple tree,
a giant's wig from his head so bald,
King Arthur's crown covered in jewels.

I will put in my box . . .
the milk from a chicken and the eggs from a cow,
the toenails of a fish and the scales of a child,
the water from a tree and the bark from a tap.

The box is made from silk woven by a gypsy,
the lock is made of fairy dresses,
the stars on the lid twinkle so bright.

It will take me to the time when dinosaurs lived,
a beach with a sea to play in with the dolphins.

Casey Trott (8)
Cwmafan Junior School, Port Talbot

The Magic Box
(Based on 'Magic Box' by Kit Wright)

I will put in my box . . .
a multicoloured charm,
a crystal rose,
a glass palace.

I will put in my box . . .
a golden unicorn,
an ice poodle,
a silver dragon.

I will put in my box . . .
a butterfly with fins,
a fish with wings,
a cat in a hat.

It is made of crystal,
stars and ice,
a rainbow,
it will take me
to the stars and Heaven.

Lois Samuel (8)
Cwmafan Junior School, Port Talbot

The River

The river is like a long plant
It's a wriggly ruler
It's a path
It's like a long, thin bath
It can be a blue shoelace that is long
It can be a stash of stones
It is like blue hair.

Ffion James-Hargreaves (8)
Cwmafan Junior School, Port Talbot

The Magic Box
(Based on 'Magic Box' by Kit Wright)

I will put in my box . . .
A golden dragon with jewels,
A silver sun,
A plague of jellyfish.

I will put in my box . . .
An elephant's trunk but multicoloured,
A purple puppy dog's tail,
A pirate's ship.

I will put in my box . . .
A camel's horns,
A cow's hump,
A chicken's milk and a goat's feather.

The box is fashioned from . . .
The scales of a snake,
The lock is a sardine's tail
And the corners are made from butter.

It will take me to the Pacific Ocean
And into the Sahara Desert
And I will get washed up
On the beach in the morning.

Lucia Edwards-Collier (9)
Cwmafan Junior School, Port Talbot

Incredible Insects

Lazy ladybird munching on a leaf,
while all the other insects settle down beneath.

Spotty little insect flying oh so high,
if he lived again I'm sure he'd touch the sky.

Sleepy little earthworm decides to take a rest,
now I've introduced him, I'm sure you'll think he's the best.

Jessica Summers (10)
Cwmafan Junior School, Port Talbot

The Magic Box
(Based on 'Magic Box' by Kit Wright)

I will put in my box . . .
The magic lamp that the genie gave me,
A glistening red rose,
My three special wishes.

I will put in my box . . .
My special, magical blanket,
My glistening best friends,
The candyfloss that was made from the clouds.

I will put in my box . . .
My mummy and daddy having a dummy,
My gran and grandad going to school,
A fish with wings.

My box is fashioned from . . .
Lots of glistening butterflies
And lots of dragons' gloomy eyes.

My box will take me to . . .
A fairy land with all my wishes and dreams.

Amelia D G Martin (8)
Cwmafan Junior School, Port Talbot

The River

The river is a glistening blue sky.
The river is a bumpy cloud.
The river is a grey snake.
The river is a blue banana.
The river is a golden glitter.
The river is a giant shoelace.
The river is a bendy ruler.
The river is an elastic band
But it is just a river.

Danielle Donovan (8)
Cwmafan Junior School, Port Talbot

A Poem About Cwmafan

In Cwmafan you can see . . .
Birds in the trees
Flowers swaying in the breeze
Children playing happily on the field.

In Cwmafan you can hear . . .
The river trickling fast
Birds singing sweetly
Car engines starting loudly
Children playing noisily.

In Cwmafan you can smell . . .
Food from the canteen
The petrol fumes from cars
Grass on the field
The lovely scent of flowers.

Rebekah Miles (9)
Cwmafan Junior School, Port Talbot

An Oxwich Sense Poem

At Oxwich I can see . . .
A huge sandy beach that runs along the rocks and cliffs.
The church standing on the mountain side.

At Oxwich I can hear . . .
Trees blowing in the wind.
Birds singing in the sky.

At Oxwich I can smell . . .
The seafood being cooked in the hotel.
The wild garlic growing in the grass.

At Oxwich I can feel . . .
The tarmac road under my feet.
Sand and stones in my shoes.

Declan Jones (8)
Cwmafan Junior School, Port Talbot

The Magic Box
(Based on 'Magic Box' by Kit Wright)

I will put in my box . . .
A magical book.
A multicoloured rose.
An all different-coloured leaf.

I will put in my box . . .
A purple diamond.
A unicorn's horn.
A red wand.

I will put in my box . . .
A wizard that has a blue cloak.
A golden apple that has fallen.
A flower.

The box is made from . . .
Magic and miracles.
It will take me to the stars and moon.

Emily MacDuff (8)
Cwmafan Junior School, Port Talbot

Happiness Is . . .

Happiness is . . .
going surfing on the beach,
learning to play the electric guitar,
playing in the sandpit.

Happiness is . . .
my parents taking me to a skateboarding park,
playing football with my cousins,
going over my friend's house.

Happiness is . . .
learning to play hockey,
making funny faces in the mirror
and playing on the ice.

Megan Baker (8)
Cwmafan Junior School, Port Talbot

A Poem About Cwmafan

In Cwmafan you can see . . .
Birds in the tree
Flowers swaying in the breeze
Children playing happily on the field.

In Cwmafan you can hear . . .
The river trickling fast
Birds singing sweetly
Car engines starting loudly
Children playing noisily.

In Cwmafan you can smell . . .
Food from the canteen
The petrol fumes from cars
Grass on the field
The lovely scent of flowers.

Aron Wilkinson (9)
Cwmafan Junior School, Port Talbot

Happiness

Happiness is when you get a funny feeling
Of mums and dads giggling and tickling.
Birds singing on summer days.
Going to the beach to paddle in the waves.
Happiness is everything.
All the spirits that life can bring.
The sound of laughter all around.
It goes through the houses and echoes through the ground.
Everyone is smiling with their gleaming faces
With gold and silver shades.

Rhianna Hughes (8)
Cwmafan Junior School, Port Talbot

The Magic Box
(Based on 'Magic Box' by Kit Wright)

I will put in my box . . .
My secret wishes and dreams,
My very own beautiful pony,
A widescreen TV.

I will put in my box . . .
My own carousel park,
My own world with fun and laughter,
All my favourite books and jewellery.

I will put in my box . . .
My best friend being Mrs Cross, my teacher,
A wizard doing schoolwork,
My headmaster having a row.

It is fashioned from . . .
Multicoloured stars, moons and planets
And imaginative coloured pictures
Made from my mind.

It will take me to history,
Back in time to 1700-1900,
Down under to discover Titanic's mysteries.

Megan Edwards (8)
Cwmafan Junior School, Port Talbot

Minibeasts

A buzzing bee
A slimy slug
A muttering moth
A lady bug

A ladybird dressed all in red,
Apart from the black spots
Around his head!

Kayleigh Robins (9)
Cwmafan Junior School, Port Talbot

The Magic Box
(Based on 'Magic Box' by Kit Wright)

I will put in my box . . .
a big pair of smelly socks,
a pair of pants,
a very small hut.

I will put in my box . . .
a battered football,
a rugby ball,
a very weird diamond.

I will put in my box . . .
an old boat,
a black star,
a golden moon.

It's made from blue,
The lid is made from sand.
It will take me to an unknown world.
It will take me to Africa.
A cuboid world.
It will take me to an underground world.

Jordan Heatman (8)
Cwmafan Junior School, Port Talbot

Moth

Moth, moth,
what do you eat
or why don't you stand on your feet?

Moth, moth,
why do you fly in the night
and try to find a little light?

Moth, moth,
why do you fly so high,
up in the breezy sky?

Benjamin Rees (9)
Cwmafan Junior School, Port Talbot

My Journey To Saturn

Gobsmacked and nervous,
I found out by letter I had won a prize.
Hooray! Yippee! I'm going to Saturn
For my prize, wahoo!

Nervous and scared as the big day arrived.
Tall and alone as I walked up to Apollo II
The rocket.

The noise of take-off was as loud as thunder
Bang, bang, bang!
Fast and furious was the speed of the take-off.

Endless as the day went by, tick-tock, tick-tock,
Fast, rush, we are on our way to Saturn, wahoo!

Beautiful and lovely
I saw Saturn for the first time ever
Saturn's a lovely beige colour,
The second biggest too.

I got so close to the planet
I had shivers going down my spine.
Finally we landed
I was the first girl to go on Saturn.

Rhian Hillier (10)
Gaer Junior School, Newport

My Brother

My brother Daniel never plays games
Really he's a big pain
He sometimes does wrestling moves on me
And he makes terrible cups of tea
My brother makes me laugh
But sometimes can be quite daft.

Lydia Slape (8)
Gaer Junior School, Newport

My Mum

My mum Sally
Likes what I do to my doll Ally
She's the best mum ever I'd say
But she gets on my nerves sometimes.

She has browny hair
But she doesn't live by the Gaer
My mum loves dogs but especially Jake
My uncle's dog.

She always does the cooking for us
But she never catches the bus
My mum will always be there for me
No matter what.

She moans and groans to my brothers
And she always tells me my name means lover
I love my mum
And I always will.

Cariad Lewis (9)
Gaer Junior School, Newport

The Minotaur

The Minotaur is very, very strong and he's very powerful.
He lives in high, dark, long caves.
His head is like a monster and he looks unbeatable.
His eyes are big, red and scary.
On the top of his head he has thorns like a bull's horn
And a goat's horn together.
His body is like a fish monster's body.
He feeds on everything alive.
He is a killer monster.
When people see him they try to run away
But the Minotaur gets them before they run away.

Curtis Macias (9)
Gaer Junior School, Newport

The Solar System

The sun is a boiling star
It keeps us warm from day till dawn.

Mysterious Mercury boiling like lava
So hot turns all to dust.

Venus the planet with chemical gases
Then it has killing acid.

Earth the greatest planet
So it should be king of them all.

Mars the planet as big as the stars
All the craters bigger than cars.

Jupiter the king of them all
All the rest are tennis balls.

Silent Saturn spins around
The planet of beauty and full of grace.

Ugly Uranus the tilted planet
With its green land full of colour.

Nasty Neptune, God of the sea
And this is the end of my solar system poem.

Thomas Holtom (10)
Gaer Junior School, Newport

The Minotaur

The Minotaur is a vicious beast
He lives in the underground
His head is like a ball of fire
His eyes are like dripping blood
On the top of his head he has horns like sharp swords
His body is wet, cold and spiky
He feeds on human flesh and souls
He is the Minotaur
When people see him they faint.

Adrienne Bartlett (9)
Gaer Junior School, Newport

A Journey To Neptune

Amazed and startled, I opened a letter to find
I'd won a prize.
Cool wicked I've won a journey to Neptune.

Excited but nervous, the big day finally arrives.
I can't believe it.
Sad but gobsmacked, I say goodbye
and slowly walk to my destiny.

Sweating and squashed I struggle into the space suit.
Overwhelmed, we are about to take off
3, 2, 1, blast-off.

I catch a glimpse of Neptune for the first time
it is extraordinary and glamorous
its colour is deep blue.

I've just landed on the planet, it's relieving but freezing,
it sends a shiver down my spine but I've arrived
at my destination.

The first girl ever to land on Neptune.
Hooray.

Samantha Reardon (10)
Gaer Junior School, Newport

A Poem About My Sister Elizabeth

My sister is sweet
And she likes meat.
She likes to go to the pool
And is so cool.

My sister rides a bike
But she doesn't ride a trike.
My sister's not a bore
But she does explore.

Bethan Rudd (8)
Gaer Junior School, Newport

Deep Dark Space

Misty sun burns night and day
And always there to make our day.

Mercury's face is red
Like a child after a race.

Venus is orange with acid inside.

Earth's a planet with creatures and clouds
Blue and green, we're third in the crowd.

Mars is the planet of war
Red as a bouncy ball.

Jupiter's moons juggle in space,
In a crowd but still in pace.

Saturn's moons dancing in space
Always keeping in perfect place.

Uranus' moons float in space
With their rings they stay in place.

Neptune floating like a dream lagoon
Always in place and always in bloom.

Pluto all alone at the back
He's the last in the pack.

Alex Blackley (10)
Gaer Junior School, Newport

My Brother Daniel

My brother Daniel is sometimes a pain
But he is very tame
He very often goes in my mum's bed
He usually wants to be fed
My brother is so funny
He makes me feel like a bunny!

Jamie Wall (8)
Gaer Junior School, Newport

My Brother Jake

My brother Jake
who acts like a snake.
Jake who always moans about his hair
then cries what he is going to wear.
Jake who's always asking for money,
but he hates honey!

Jake likes to play with the ball
then always jumps people's walls.

Jake is always sliding down people's banks
but he never comes home in a tank.
He's always out on the street,
but he never has dirty feet!

Jake likes to play with the cars
but he never watches the TV stars.
Jake never eats his food,
he'll never a make a cool dude!

Ryan Young (8)
Gaer Junior School, Newport

My Journey To Mars

Nervous and surprised, I opened the letter to find out I'd got a prize,
I was astonished and gobsmacked that it was a journey to Mars.

Heart pounding and scared the big day arrived.
Shocked and amazed I see the rocket for the first time.

Struggling, I put on the heavy, gleaming space suit.
The fast and furious speed of the rocket hurtles through the sky.

I caught a glimpse of the red surface of Mars.
As we came closer I saw large craters and red sand.

I was relieved and exhausted that we had landed.
I was the first boy on Mars.

It was weeks of slow travelling and got quite boring.
It was superb and extremely exciting!

Jamie Reed (10)
Gaer Junior School, Newport

Planet Poem

Steamy sun is very bright
With a huge, yellow, misty light

Mini Mercury is so bright
If you lived on there you'd have a fright

Violent Venus will destroy our lives
The acid cloud will melt our eyes

Earth is blue like a sea of glue
Earth is green like a wet, grassy green

Mars is full of craters dusty and red
If you fall off you will be dead.

Giant Jupiter is big and red
It's bigger than my king-sized bed.

Smelly Saturn is sixth in line
It's full of gases but I don't mind.

Unique Uranus is aqua in colour
I've never seen anything nicer.

Nasty Neptune is blue as the sea
When I look up I can see me.

Playing Pluto is last in line
It's silver in colour but shines and shines.

Aimee Hunt (10)
Gaer Junior School, Newport

My Brother

My brother is a pain
He is so lame
He boogies all night
And has fights
And in the morning
He looks like he's flown a kite
All night!

Ellis Chapman (8)
Gaer Junior School, Newport

The Nine Planets

The sun is a big ball of spice!
Shining by day and in the sparkle of night.

Mighty Mercury is so hot,
if you sat in its craters, you'd think it was a frying pot.

Vile Venus is like a ball of burning acid gas
Venus is like an orange floating in space.

Exhilarating Earth is holding hostages in Iraq!
Earth can be dangerous, but also can be peaceful.

Miniature Mars is half the size of Earth
but it's as shiny as a red apple.

Jetty Jupiter, big and round as a giant red eye
watching meteors shoot through space.

Snooker Saturn has 20 more snooker balls
than Earth's snooker table.

Underground Uranus is a mystery
spinning rings on its side.

Nippy Neptune, made of gas
with rings that are peculiar and dark.

Puny Pluto is so small, it's like a puppy dog
that you could adore!

Ryan Cox (10)
Gaer Junior School, Newport

My Dad

My dad is a king
My dad is the best of all dads
My dad is 42
My dad drinks beer and ends up drunk
My dad sleeps.

Nathan Williams (8)
Gaer Junior School, Newport

A Journey To Mars

Excited and surprised I found I had won a prize in the mail.
Nervous but joyful, I read the letters and found I was going to Mars.

I woke up scared and worried, the day had finally arrived
Frightened and nervous, I saw the rocket for the first time,
It was huge.

Happy but nervous I squeezed into the shiny space suit
Worried, I heard 3 . . . 2 . . . 1 . . .
The speed of the rocket was fast and furious.

The days are going slowly but it has been fun
Talking to my family on Earth and pressing buttons.
Cramped and squashed, it is hard to breathe and move.

I caught sight of the beautiful red planet, Mars,
You can see the rocky surface,
The bright stars and its unbearable heat.

Landed! I am so tired and relieved to be off the rocket.
I am the first boy on Mars.

Mark Goddard (10)
Gaer Junior School, Newport

The Minotaur

The Minotaur is an ugly, long-toothed beast
He lives in a very confusing windy cave that no one can escape from
His head is like a cat that has just got out of the washing machine
His eyes are like big red buttons
On the top of his head he has horns like sharp knives
His body is as fat as a really big elephant
He feeds on human flesh
He is a nasty piece of work
When people see him they run to their homes, crying in fright.

Abigail Coe (9)
Gaer Junior School, Newport

A Journey To Venus

Surprised and amazed I read my text to say I had won the prize.
Hooray! Bingo! I've won a trip to Venus.

Nervous and scared the big day finally arrived.
I was startled and gobsmacked at the size of the rocket.

I struggled to squeeze into the heavy and expensive space suit.
Hurtling and being catapulted, we zoomed through the air,
We were travelling really fast.

Slowly and boring we travel,
Through very exciting and very occupying
Bullet-like and very fast we fly through the air.

Peering through space I saw the beautiful sight of Venus.
Shocked and surprised, I saw Venus had no moons.

Relieved and shattered we finally touched down on Venus.
The first girl on Venus, my mission complete.

Emily Carver (10)
Gaer Junior School, Newport

The Solar System

The sun is like a burning fire which shines
through the night like a giant light.

Magic Mercury, craters all around
leaves a mark in its mighty light.

Venus, Venus has acid clouds
which can burn through your flesh.

Exotic Earth so full of life
so many seas and swaying with trees
with little honeybees.

Mini Mars is full of war
little red Martians begin on the floor.

Giant Jupiter the colour of the sunset
and a rosy-red nose.

Christopher Williams (10)
Gaer Junior School, Newport

Faraway Planets

Super sun
Bright as light
Even shining in the night.

Magical Mercury
Fireball bright
Sparkle up well in the night.

Venus is next to Earth
Full of acid
And yellow, burning gases.

Our planet we live on
Is the one that's best
It's green and blue
With one moon.

Magic Mars
Big and red
Big, huge craters
Like a bed.

Just Jupiter
Has got a spot on its face
Always keeping in perfect pace.

Spicy Saturn
With rings on its face
It looks like crystal lace.

Unicorn Uranus
Blue as blue can be
It reminds me of the sea.

Neptune's blue
Like a lagoon
And it's shaped like a balloon.

Pluto is dark
Like its moon
And it's nothing like a lagoon.

Jade Windsor (10)
Gaer Junior School, Newport

The Story Of The Planets

Scorching sun is one of the stars
It's way bigger than dusty, red Mars

Mini Mercury is so hot
Almost roasted by the sun

Venomous Venus has so much danger
Just like a nasty army major

Earth has such strange weather
Like all the planets mixed together

Murderous Mars is the God of war
Its colour is bloodstained red

Jupiter is the biggest ball
It is the king of all

Saturn is so vain
Its rings are made of ice

Uranus is a ball of gas
It is like a blue balloon

Nasty Neptune is as dark as the night
It's far away from bright white light

Puny Pluto is covered in ice
It's so far away, so that's the end of my poem.

Matthew Perrin (11)
Gaer Junior School, Newport

The Solar System

Super sun is brilliant with its heat
it is spectacular, it's so neat.

Mighty Mercury is a double of the sun
it will amaze you and you will be astounded.

Vile Venus is a danger to all
it burns acid so fast and stands so tall.

Earth so quiet and peaceful
it floats, spectacular like a balloon.

Mars as red as a snooker ball
shining on space's table.

Jupiter like a cold, icy river
flowing.

Saturn's rings glow with ice and sparkle brightly
as the moons dance round.

Uranus is gold like a gold
shooting star.

Neptune is far away from the sun
a very cold, icy planet.

Pluto, as blue as the night sky
it's like the ocean itself and so calm.

Matthew Thorn (10)
Gaer Junior School, Newport

The Planet Poem

Steamy sun is yellow, so bright
It shines through the moon at night.

Mighty Mercury is so hot
If you land on it you will *pop*.

Venomous Venus is made of gas
You could cook a whole class.

Earth has got blue seas
And also got a lot of bees

Mysterious Mars
Is like a chocolate bar.

Jumping Jupiter juggles its moons.

Saturn, like a helium orange balloon.

Uranus is not happy
Because it is so gassy.

Neptune is blue like seas
But has no trees or bumblebees.

Pluto is the tiniest
And that is the end of my great big poem.

James Morgan (11)
Gaer Junior School, Newport

Planet Mania

Mercury, Mercury is hotter than an oven,
It will pop over a dozen.

Venus is the goddess of love
And is as sweet as a dove.

Earth owns me
And is a tiny speck of a micro bee.

Red old Mars,
Can see shooting stars.

Boys go to Jupiter to get more *stupider,*
Girls go to college to get more knowledge.

Saturn has the rings,
Thirteen that is.

Uranus is vivid
And has no one there to be livid.

Neptune is as blue as
An ocean lagoon.

Pluto is cold and small
And is a sphere, like a ball.

Sophie Gillard (11)
Gaer Junior School, Newport

The Solar System

Sun is yellow with glaring colours
it shines up in the sky.

Magical Mercury is small and bright
and gets hotter every night.

Venomous Venus with acid gas
is like a bell of smoke.

Earth is as blue as the sea
and green as the shining grass
you will see.

Mysterious Mars is red as an apple
and dusty as it goes by.

Jumping Jupiter is like a snooker ball
and ball of fire.

Secret Saturn is yellow
with slimy rings around it.

Uranus has a spinning ring
on his side.

Neptune is blue, like the sea
with black rings around it.

Pluto is the smallest planet
and dark as it will ever be.

Harriet Oliver (10)
Gaer Junior School, Newport

All About Space

Super sun is big and bright
which you can't miss day and night.

Magical Mercury small and bright
full of craters day and night.

Violent Venus that burns you alive
because of that you won't survive.

Excellent Earth full of life
which no other planet will be like.

Misty Mars is dusty and red
if you fall off you will be dead.

Giant Jupiter is like a big ball of fire
which won't hurt you or won't go higher.

Secret Saturn is big and round
if you fall off you won't hit the ground.

Uranus looks turquoise
you can almost see it in your eyes.

Nipper Neptune as blue as the sea
I love swimming with you and me.

Playing Pluto so dusty and dark
it is not as evil as a shark.

Ameen Hail (10)
Gaer Junior School, Newport

The Planets

Solar sun is like a ball of light
giving life to everyone.

Mini Mercury is a fiery hell
racing like a Mazda MR2.

Venomous Venus has acid
on every single bit of the planet.

Earth is a place where
we laze around all day.
As blue as the sea god, Neptune.

Mars is known as the red planet
like jolly Jupiter, proud to be
best of the rest.

Saturn's aliens race around its icy rings.

Ugly Uranus as calm as the sun.

Neptune is a blue, dreamy lagoon.

Pimply Pluto is the smallest and coldest.

Kieran Farr (11)
Gaer Junior School, Newport

A Trip To Venus

I was shocked and amazed when I found out I'd won a prize
by opening the letter.
I was amazed and startled, I had won a trip to Venus.
Excited and nervous, the day eventually arrived.
I saw the huge rocket for the first time.
It was a struggle as I put my space suit on as the noise
of the rocket was outstanding.
After days of travelling I caught a glimpse of Venus.
Then the captain said, 'Contact - the Eagle has landed.'

Scott Mullen (10)
Gaer Junior School, Newport

My Journey To Uranus

Shocked and surprised
I got a big letter winning a cool prize
I don't know how
It was a free trip to icy Uranus, holy cow!

The day arrived, I was nervous and scared,
What would happen
I got to the big, huge, black rocket
And wondered if it was a sham.

I put the white, gleaming suit on as I blasted into the sky.
I zoomed into space, speeding along I said, 'Bye-bye!'

I slowly made my way through deep, dark space,
Suddenly we went fast and furious, this was a better pace.

It was beautiful, I saw it . . . Uranus! In all its watery goodness!
Inside the shimmering water I saw a black core of rock and ice!

On the icy cold surface I landed and floated on Uranus' water,
Relieved and exhausted I realised that I was the first boy on Uranus . . .
Then I went surfing!

Will D Court (10)
Gaer Junior School, Newport

I've Got A Ry Ry

I've got a Ry Ry
Behind my curtains,
Fierce as dragons,
Spiny and horrible,
His eyes are brown,
His teeth are small and sharp,
His tail is long,
Nose prickly!
Bum spotty,
I've got a Ry Ry
Which comes out at night and
Gives my nan a fright!

Lewis Wylie (8)
Gaer Junior School, Newport

The Planets Of The Solar System

Hot sun is like a ball, fiery and tall.

Mercury is hot and is a tiny tot.

Venus has no life you will have to strive
to survive.

Super Earth has given birth to life.

The moon is like a big balloon
that is the Earth's possession.

Red Mars, bringer of war,
is like the wild and fierce boar.

Jupiter is grander because it is
the greatest.

Saturn is acid and so are the clouds.

Rocky Uranus is dangerous to
any human being.

Neptune's sea is as great as
the great blue whale.

Pluto is tiny and last of them all.
This is my solar system poem.

Richard Hills (10)
Gaer Junior School, Newport

The Solar System

Sunburnt sun shines up the solar system.

Mini Mercury zooms like a Ferrari in space.

Vain Venus is as hot as the Roman goddess of love.

Earth is the place we'll never leave.

Mighty Mars might be inhabited by puny Earthlings.

Giant Jupiter and his moons are a gang of crooks,
but the cosmic cops can't catch them.

Show-off Saturn likes to show off its shining rings.

Unusual Uranus spins head over heels
like a bowling ball in space.

Neptune's as blue as the deep blue sea.

Puny Pluto, as small as our moon
(and Charon's even smaller).

Fedor Tot (10)
Gaer Junior School, Newport

The Planets

The sun is a shining star,
The prettiest star by far.

Mercury is very hot,
It's grown too big for its cot.

Venus is second in line,
Soon it will be mine.

Earth is manic,
It needs a mechanic.

Mars is fourth,
It sadly is a dwarf.

Boys go to Jupiter,
To get more *stupider*.

Saturn is very pretty,
A shame it isn't witty.

Uranus is known,
Because it is famous.

Neptune is a blue colour,
Sadly it doesn't have a mother.

Pluto is last,
But that doesn't mean it's fast.

Charlotte Shadbolt (11)
Gaer Junior School, Newport

Perfect Planets

Sun is the star shining so bright,
All the other planets gaze in delight.

Mysterious Mercury moves all night
It's near to the sun so it's very bright.

Venomous Venus has an acid bite,
It would give a snake quite a fright.

Earth has weather like sun and rain,
It's full of happiness and pain.

Mars is like a red fiery ball,
We don't know whether it's big or small.

Jupiter can fit every planet inside,
And there's still more room for us to hide.

Saturn shines like a disco ball,
It would never crash and fall.

Uranus is so dark and grey,
If you look hard it will fade away.

Neptune's as dark as the sea in the night,
It's far away from light and bright.

Puny Pluto is like a snooker ball,
If there was no gravity it would be the first to fall.

Bethan Maye (10)
Gaer Junior School, Newport

A Journey To Pluto

Amazed and stunned I had a letter saying that I had won a prize.
Hooray! I'd won a trip to Pluto!

Shaky but confident the day finally arrived.
Stiff and terrified I walked up to the giant rocket.

I tried to pop into the rubbery glittering space suit.
The speed of the rocket went like a bullet soaring through the air.

Tired and bored of being in a rocket for days
We were gradually getting there.
Like a roller coaster but as fast as a bullet
Oh I thought I was going to be sick.

I caught a tiny glimpse of the crystal glowing planet Pluto.
As I got closer it was like a silver metal ball.

I landed on the planet I couldn't believe my eyes
I was shattered and relieved.

I was the first girl on Pluto
Now I'd be famous . . .

Sophie Calland (10)
Gaer Junior School, Newport

I've Got A Wooga Wooga

We've got a Wooga Wooga in our basement,
He's as clumsy as an elephant,
My sister Natalie doesn't believe in Wooga Wooga,
His mouth is as big as a size 9 football,
His feet are bigger than his body,
Wooga Wooga nose is smaller than a rubber,
His arms are as long as the Twin Towers,
He is as fierce as a buffalo,
Wooga Wooga is as fast as a jumbo jet,
I've got a Wooga Wooga in my basement,
He is like family to me.

James Luckett (8)
Gaer Junior School, Newport

My Journey To Pluto

I felt excited and lucky when I found out
I had won a prize.
Fainted, worried I'd won a trip to Pluto.

Amazing, worried, the day came and I was really nervous.
Huge and white, there it was so big and so lonely,
The big rocket.

Heavy and cramped I squeezed in my suit
And plodded along the platform. Three, two, one!
The engines powered and I catapulted towards Pluto.

Slowly but amazingly I got there.
I had a lot to do.
Furious and mean, I flew so fast yet so slow.

Amazed when I saw the first sight of Pluto.
Freezing, the planet sent shivers down my spine
We landed and it was a relief to get on the surface.

The first boy on Pluto.

Joel Kennedy (10)
Gaer Junior School, Newport

My Nan

This is a poem about my nan
She does not sew but my grandad tows a caravan,
My nan's alive and she's 55,
And always makes me laugh,
My nan is so kind, I think she's fine,
She gives me money and is very funny.
She does not smoke,
But has a joke,
They are always twice as funny,
My nan is good at talking, but not very good at walking!

Joshua Wood (8)
Gaer Junior School, Newport

A Journey To Earth

Shocked and stunned.
I've got a letter in the post informing me I've won a prize.
I am nervous but glad. I've won a trip to Earth.

I am scared and worried but the day is finally here.
I am terrified and sad. I have seen the rocket. It is so cool!

The space suit is heavy and plain. I have a struggle to get into it.
As I take off I am so excited. The speed of the rocket is so fast.

I am so bored, yet excited. This is so cool.
All of the planets flash by. This is so cool.
The rocket is so fast I feel a little sick.

Amazingly I catch a glimpse of the beautiful planet Earth.
I draw near to the blue and white planet.

I am very tired. I have landed, finally.
I am the first alien on Earth.

Amy Turner (10)
Gaer Junior School, Newport

I've Got A Hal Hal

I've got a Hal Hal
Who scares me every night,
He's slippery and slimy,
He's very smelly, cor blimey!
He never washes,
He's as enormous as a house,
Only I can see my Hal Hal,
He waits under the stairs,
Gives my brother a scare,
Boo! *Off with your head!*
He follows me everywhere,
He thinks I'm the real deal,
You can't blame him for being nasty,
He's Henry VIII's ghost!

Aaron Monkley (8)
Gaer Junior School, Newport

My Journey To Saturn

I was startled and amazed as I opened a letter
That said I'd won a prize,
Stunned and joyful, I'd won a trip to Saturn.

My spine shivered, my teeth clattered, the big day had come,
Tall and alone stood zero 6 in all its glory,
I felt fear strike me, I was petrified.

The suit was huge and shiny like tin foil,
I had to dive in like an Olympic swimmer,
The speed of the rocket was like a shot of a bullet,
And was as noisy as my class.

Endless and cramped, but lots to do,
The conditions are poor but we have an
Extraordinary view of the engine.

The stunning rings of Saturn caught my eye,
The big yellow planet, I could see all the moons and
The rings were beautiful.

The capsule stopped next to the rings,
I was exhausted and the journey had finished,
I was the first boy on Saturn.

Christopher Powell (10)
Gaer Junior School, Newport

I've Got A We We

I've got a We We in my cupboard,
Slippy and slimy,
Ever so dirty,
Lumpy and humpy,
Ever so dumpy,
Never grumpy,
If you are nasty,
My We We will blast you!
I've got a We We so look out!

Kurtis Ormond Crighton (8)
Gaer Junior School, Newport

The Planets

Silent sun shines so bright,
It's hard to be missed day or night.

Misty Mercury puts up a fight,
As it hovers through the night.

Victorious Venus full of burning acid.

Energetic Earth full of plants,
To the great white sharks to the tiny ants.

Missionless Mars keeps its pace
As it shines through space.

Jolly Jupiter gives some glances,
As it dances like a graceful butterfly.

Speedy Saturn keeps its pattern,
As it moves like an ice skater in space.

Upset Uranus filled with bad gas,
So many moons, there's more than a class.

Nasty Neptune as blue as a whale,
You can see it without fail.

Patient Pluto is like ice,
I wouldn't go there - that's my advice.

Lauren Hillier (10)
Gaer Junior School, Newport

Nine Planets Around The Sun

First is the sun that brightens our day,
Orange and yellow and never grey.

Next is Mercury second in line,
After the sun first of nine.

Venus is third, a ball of acid light,
Next to the Earth and very bright.

Earth is next, it has one moon,
Our world we love and care for too.

Mars is fourth, red and round,
It has craters on the ground.

Jupiter juggles its moons in space,
It also has a spot on its face.

Saturn is a ball of colour,
Which is red and many others.

Uranus is seventh, a blue lagoon,
Is a blue ball, that has no moon.

Neptune's next covered in blue,
It also has more than eight moons.

Pluto is last, furthest away,
We might find more another day.

Hannah Snelling (10)
Gaer Junior School, Newport

The Fantastic Planets

Fantastic sun is a flaming star,
The hotness from Earth is now by far.

Midgy Mercury is very small,
Is a very bright round ball.

Fabulous Venus is so bright,
Full of acids and full of light.

Electrical Earth, three quarters water,
Water is like the deep blue sea.

Magical Mars is known for the red planet,
With craters deep as can be.

Only Jupiter has got a spot,
His rings are stones, ice and rocks.

Snooker ball Saturn has eighteen moons or more,
Swirling around like a twirling whizzing ball.

Unique Uranus is on its side,
Full of gas like a helium balloon.

Neptune is a stunning blue colour, swaying in the gusty wind,
All the planet is water.

Tiny Pluto the smallest planet,
Very dark, far from the sun.

Annalize James (10)
Gaer Junior School, Newport

The Wonderful Solar System

Flaming sun, biggest star in the solar system,
Gives heat to all nine planets.

Magial Mercury is boiling hot,
Very small and very bright.

Vicious Venus is full of acid,
Fabulous orange burns all day.

Earth is full of water and land,
The only planet with flaming life.

Mighty Mars full of craters,
Like a giant juicy orange.

Juggling Jupiter has loads of moons,
Juggles them while orbiting the sun.

Skating Saturn has rings of all colours,
The planet of beauty and full of grace.

Unique Uranus has nothing but gas,
Tilted planet and very bright.

Neptune is a big blue sea,
Full of water and frost free.

Peaceful Pluto is the ninth planet,
Smaller than Earth's moon.

Laura Emily Hardwick (10)
Gaer Junior School, Newport

A Journey To Mars

I was excited and amazed when I heard
On the telephone that I'd won a prize,
I was nervous and stunned but happy,
I was going on a trip to Mars.

The big day was finally here,
I was worried and happy, I was going to my favourite planet,
As I walked towards the launch pad, I thought, *this is cool
And awesome, I am looking at a real live rocket.*

Scared and worried as I was about to go on the rocket,
I had one last look but we were going,
The rocket was fast and furious but we were soon out of sight.

We spent days and days travelling but it was fun
And cool, never did it get boring,
The rocket was speeding and amazing but
We were real close.

It was beautiful and amazing, we had landed,
It felt great and scary, I was the first boy on Mars.

Ben Williams (10)
Gaer Junior School, Newport

I've Got A Ja Ja

I've got a Ja Ja in my house,
Mouth as big as a tunnel,
Sharp teeth to bite you in half,
Nose hairy, eyes are scary,
Five legs, no hair,
Sharp teeth, so behave!
I've got a Ja Ja so be scared,
When he's mad, he's bad,
But in the end, he'll be your friend,
Everyone is scared of him, but he loves you.

Sam Gillard (8)
Gaer Junior School, Newport

A Journey To Mercury

Excited but nervous, I had found I had won a prize by mail,
Shock and surprised, it was a journey to Mercury,
Nervous and scared, the big day finally arrived,
Shocked and amazed at how big the rocket was,
I was struggling to put the gleaming white space suit on,
As fast as lightning I zoomed into space,
I caught a glimpse of the beautiful planet Mercury
                            for the very first time.
As I got closer Mercury looked like a big grey bowling ball,
I landed on the beautiful planet of Mercury,
It was a bumpy landing,
I couldn't believe it,
I was the first girl in history to land on Mercury.

Jenna Pullen (10)
Gaer Junior School, Newport

I've Got A Cha Cha

I've got a Cha Cha in the kitchen,
And he's much, much bigger than a kitten,
He's wiggly and wiry,
Slippy and slimy,
Arms wibbly and wobbly,
As a worm with no body,
Everyone is afraid,
They all say Cha Cha's to blame,
But he is very kind,
And I do not mind!
Big brown eyes,
Perhaps if I wash him clean,
I've got a Cha Cha with shiny wings,
Every night my Cha Cha sings.

Sophie Harding (9)
Gaer Junior School, Newport

My Journey To Jupiter

Happy and nervous I answered the phone,
I heard I'd won a prize,
Confused and gobsmacked I won a trip to Jupiter.

Dizzy and shivering the day had finally come,
I was going to Jupiter,
Sad but scared I saw my first glimpse of the rocket.

Heavy and weighed down, I slid into the space suit,
The noise was too much to handle, 3, 2, 1, take-off!
It was fast and furious.

Endless and squashed, it felt like we were going nowhere,
Amazed and cramped, I was really excited about Jupiter.

I saw my first glimpse of the stunning planet
In the corner of my eye,
Jupiter was a brilliant planet, the yellow and orange planet glowed.

We finally landed, I was tired and exhausted,
Gobsmacked and nervous, I was the first boy on Jupiter.

Jordan Watkins (10)
Gaer Junior School, Newport

I've Got A Giant Horned Dog

I've got a giant horned dog,
As strong as a rhino but as gentle as an ant,
Cute and sweet and ever so neat and shiny,
Gentle and warm-hearted, caring and huggable but . . .
Watch out! When he's angry, his huge tail
Could hit you.
Eyes big and soppy, paws all hairy,
Nose sniffy, claws shiny.
I've got a giant horned dog,
When he's angry, he'll lower his horns
And *Wham! Bam! Oh no!*

Cherie Crighton
Gaer Junior School, Newport

My Journey To Venus

Amazed and shocked that I heard on the telephone,
That I had won a prize.

There was a trip to Venus.

The day had arrived, as nervous as ever
And my bones were shaking.

In amazement as I saw the Apollo I
I was gobsmacked, it was huge.

Feeling confused, I got into a snowy-white suit,
Then I was zooming off into space.

Bored stiff, as I was cramped in the space shuttle,
Amazing as I saw the great planet Venus.

Venus is a rocky planet and its colours are grey and brown.

We have landed on Venus, I am the first boy on Venus.

Michael Jones (10)
Gaer Junior School, Newport

I've Got A Chi Chi

I've got a Chi Chi in my garden shed,
As scary as an alien, face all red,
Spiky and squashy,
Curly and spotty,
Bold and brave,
I've got a Chi Chi in my shed,
Wings long and thick,
Antenna like a curly stick,
Squashy big bum,
And its tail, oh Mum!
I've got a Chi Chi, comes in the day,
Scares me and Mummy right away.

Emily Powell (8)
Gaer Junior School, Newport

A Journey To Neptune

Gobsmacked and happy
I opened the letter, I'd won a prize,
Excited and lucky, I'd won a trip to Neptune.

Nervous but excited, the day had finally arrived,
Happy but confused, I saw the rocket.

I struggled and squeezed into a heavy space suit,
Fast as lightning it was as loud as an elephant,
As we slowly took off.

Slow but amazing, the clock was ticking by,
The rocket was travelling to Neptune
Fast but furious, speeding up closer, so fast as a bullet.

I got a glimpse of Neptune and I was really shocked
Because it was blue.
I got a glimpse of Neptune, it was glamorous.

Relieved but cold we had just landed,
I was the first girl on Neptune.
Mission complete!

Natalie Luckett (11)
Gaer Junior School, Newport

I've Got A Ry Ry

I've got a Ry Ry in my wardrobe,
He scares my dog,
He eats my homework, sorry Miss!
Huge blue eyes,
A nasty, green surprise,
Watches telly,
Likes to stuff his belly,
I've got a Ry Ry, watch out,
He might eat you!

Thomas Williams (8)
Gaer Junior School, Newport

My Journey To Jupiter

I was gobsmacked and overwhelmed as I opened the letter,
I was joyful and startled that I had won a trip to Jupiter.

Scared and nervous, the day had come, I drove up to the rocket,
I saw the rocket for the first time, I felt proud and lucky.

Struggling to squeeze into the shiny, silver space suit
but it was too small,
the noise of take-off, the rocket hissed and blasted into the blue sky.

An endless, tiring journey all the way from Earth
to big old Jupiter, the speed of the rocket was
as fast as the speed of light.

Peering through the window, the extraordinary planet
Jupiter was there,
shocked and freaked, I came right over big, orange, yellow Jupiter.

Exhausted I landed on Jupiter onto its big mass
of landing ground, excited, I was the first boy on the
big orange planet of Jupiter.

Tom Wilkins (11)
Gaer Junior School, Newport

I've Got A Ry Ry

I've got a Ry Ry who lives in my house,
Fierce as a dragon,
Wild as a horse,
Fat and sloppy,
Breathing fire,
Eyes big and brown,
Teeth large and pointy,
Nose long as Pinocchio's,
I've got a Ry Ry.

Gareth Morgan (8)
Gaer Junior School, Newport

A Journey To Saturn

Gobsmacked and nervous, I found I had
Won a prize with a letter.
I was thrilled.

I was going to Saturn, nervous but excited,
The big day finally arrived, like a flash.

The great white rocket gleamed before my eyes,
I got on the tall white creation.

The fast and furious licking flames
Came from the powerful engine.

The unimaginable rocket went on and on and
One shooting star flew past, we were in space,
It was glorious.

It took my breath away, slowly I took a deep
But soft breath and stepped onto Saturn.

It looked like a red-hot volcano,
I tried to find the end of the unwinding planet,
It would not come, I was on cloud nine
Or should I say Saturn.

Ellie Dollery (10)
Gaer Junior School, Newport

I've Got A Cha Cha

I've got a Cha Cha in my bedroom,
He is as fierce as a dragon,
He breathes hotter than a cooker,
His eyes are as wild as a lion's,
But he can be as gentle as a mouse,
Watch out!
Cha Cha will gobble you up!
I've got a Cha Cha please beware,
He will eat anyone who is nasty.

Zaine Said (8)
Gaer Junior School, Newport

A Journey To Neptune

Amazed and nervous I got an e-mail,
I was stunned and confused, I'd won a journey to Neptune.

The day has arrived, I am surprised and startled,
By the massive Apollo II gleaming in the sun.

I am putting on the milky white suit slowly and calmly,
The noise and speed was faster than a hurtling bullet.

Endlessly excited we travelled around for weeks,
The cramped hot air is tiring.

I caught a glimpse of the cloudy planet Neptune,
I was shocked and gobsmacked, I saw a dark
                                bruise on Neptune.

We were landing on the cloudy and strange planet Neptune,
I was exhausted and tired, I was the first boy on
                                the beautiful Neptune.

Lincoln Baker (10)
Gaer Junior School, Newport

I've Got A Mo Mo

I've got a Mo Mo in my house,
As fat as a cow,
I don't know how,
He's as scary as a werewolf,
Teeth sharp,
He plays the harp,
Hair spiky,
Ginormous red eyes, look out!
My mum doesn't like him,
But he's fine with me,
I've got a Mo Mo who appears every Christmas,
With a present for me.

Sheldon Campbell-White (8)
Gaer Junior School, Newport

A Journey To Saturn

I was excited and gobsmacked, I had an e-mail
That said I had won a prize,
The prize was a journey to Saturn, I was nervous and worried.

The day had finally arrived, I was scared but joyful,
I saw the rocket, it was humungous, the first time I saw it
I felt sad and confused.

I was struggling and squeezing into the shiny white space suit,
The rocket was zooming off, I was glued to the seat.

Endless time, it seemed like forever, as we travelled
Through space, but never bored - lots to do.

I was excited and happy to see the beautiful planet of
Saturn for the first time,
It was huge, yellow with rings made from ice and dust.

The rocket finally landed with a bump,
I was the first person on Saturn.

Lauren Nicola Maggs (10)
Gaer Junior School, Newport

I've Got A Ma Ma

I've got a Ma Ma in my attic,
His eyes are massive (bigger than tennis balls),
His mouth oh - blimey is like a cave,
Legs long and slimy,
Claws as pointy as metal blades,
He's got a tattoo that fades,
Tail all pointy and fat,
Teeth as sharp as a rat,
He awakens at night
And gives my family a fright,
I've got a Ma Ma in my attic,
Beware when you're up there!

Ben Ford-Weaver (8)
Gaer Junior School, Newport

A Journey To Neptune

I was gobsmacked and shocked when I got an e-mail
Nervous and lucky I won a prize to Neptune.

The big day came, I finally saw a rocket, it was ginormous,
My teeth were clattering and my legs were shaking.

Freaked and confused, I couldn't get into my special space suit,
Till an hour later when I had help from the others to get me into it.

Endless and a tiring ride, I have been travelling for a day,
The rocket was burning like a volcano erupting.

Surprised and stunned, Neptune caught my eagle eye,
Shocked and weird, I saw a dark bruise on Neptune.

We finally landed, Neptune and its moon were petrifying,
I was the first boy on Neptune.
Mission accomplished!

Harry Price (10)
Gaer Junior School, Newport

I've Got A Moo Moo

I've got a Moo Moo in my back garden,
As scary as a dragon,
As quiet as a mouse,
Claws huge and sharp - oh no!
Mouth as large as the Severn Bridge,
One-eyed cyclops,
Tall as a tower,
Green alien being,
Bum all bumpy,
Ears all pusy,
I've got a Moo Moo who likes to scare my sister,
But is kind to me.

Kyle McCarthy (8)
Gaer Junior School, Newport

The Journey To Saturn

I was gobsmacked and nervous,
I had just won a prize,
The prize was a journey to Saturn,
Let's celebrate, hooray!

Suffering with fright, the big day had finally arrived,
I was amazed at the huge rocket,
I was terrified with fright.

Then I had to squeeze my way into
The shiny silver space suit.

It gleamed with a coating of a creamy-white,
Then we went into the wonderful rocket,
Wow! I gasped with amazement.

There was a million buttons on the control panel.

Then the driver said, 'Up and away',
The sound was squealing.
It was spinning me round,
It was like a roller coaster.

It was an everlasting ride,
It went on and on and on.

Scary but good it was *cool!*

Carys Barnett (10)
Gaer Junior School, Newport

Love And Hate

Love is red,
Hate is black,
Love is time whipping by,
Hate is Hell rushing back,
Love is angels flying in the air,
Hate is a clock going anticlockwise,
I love you but you hate me.

Danielle Hirons (9)
Garnteg Primary School, Pontypool

What Is White?

What is white? A kite is white,
Blowing in the breeze at night.

What is blue? My shoe is blue,
After I have polished it through.

What is gold? My locket is gold,
With my initials standing bold.

What is red? My bed is red,
Where I'm sleeping with ted.

What is cream? My pillow is cream,
Where I'm led down having a dream.

What is turquoise? A clock is turquoise,
With its hands spinning clockwise.

Keelley Quigley (10)
Garnteg Primary School, Pontypool

What Is Red?

What is red? A rose is red,
Its petals falling on my bed.

What is green? The trees are green,
Swaying in the summer breeze.

What is white? The stars are white,
Glistening all through the night.

What is blue? The sea is blue,
That the dolphins swim through.

What is gold? The sun is gold,
Shining bright and bold.

Jade Cox (10)
Garnteg Primary School, Pontypool

What Is Red?

What is red? A bulldog ant is red,
Stinging whatever may tread.

What is green? A grasshopper's green,
Sitting in the emerald green.

What is peach? A worm is peach,
Escaping the nasty bleach.

What is brown? Wings of a butterfly are brown,
Fluttering in the air without sound.

What is grey? A woodlouse is grey,
Curling up under wood and clay.

What is black? A spider is black,
Sitting in a fly-catching sack.

What is violet? A ground beetle is violet,
Standing in the sunbeam's twilight.

What is gold? A scarab beetle is gold,
Eating whenever warm or cold.

Liam Lewis (10)
Garnteg Primary School, Pontypool

Colours

Red is like a rose,
Blowing in the wind,
Yellow is round like the glowing sun,
Green is like the beautiful grass,
Blowing in the wind,
Orange is like the sun,
Leaving the sky,
Blue is like waves crashing into the rocks,
White is like the clouds floating in the air.

Lauren Harris (9)
Garnteg Primary School, Pontypool

From A Spaceship

Faster than meteors, faster than stars,
Neptune, Saturn and tiny Earth cars,
And moving along like a jet in the sky,
All through space you're waiting to fly,
All of the sights of the planets in space,
Since we took off it's been a race
And ever again in the flash of the sun
You are waiting to land on Saturn.

Here is a spaceship that zooms at high speed,
All by itself it's bombing its seas,
Here is an alien that stands and waits,
And here are its enemies that it hates,
Here is a spaceman floating in space,
Cuts off his cords and lands flat on his face,
And here is the red planet that they call Mars,
As we drive past, it is surrounded by stars.

Jordan White (10)
Garnteg Primary School, Pontypool

Fear

Fear is black
Like a bottomless pit,
Everyone gets frightened,
Now and then it comes
And goes no one
Knows when.
Fear is a deadly blade,
Coming to stab you,
Or something stuck
In your throat and you
Can't get it out,
You can fear spiders, crickets
Or other creepy-crawlies,
But you all know what you fear.

Callum Roynon (9)
Garnteg Primary School, Pontypool

Anger

Anger is like an alligator,
Chomping you,
Fire in your eyes,
Steam launching out of your ears,
Roaring at the wind,
As red as blood,
Brain is bursting out fire,
Chomping food as hard as possible,
Screaming your eyes out!

Holly Parker (9)
Garnteg Primary School, Pontypool

The Beach

The water is shimmering and glistening
Like diamonds,
Waves are splashing,
And banging against the water,
The sand is boiling hot,
As hot as a kettle,
The sun is shining,
Like a big torch.

Kirstie Mayley (10)
Garnteg Primary School, Pontypool

Birds

Birds are little animals,
Their eyes are like black ladybirds,
They have colourful tails,
Their wings are like thick sticks,
Flitting in the air,
Their beaks are like razors.

Tara Earnshaw (9)
Garnteg Primary School, Pontypool

Taz The Dog

Taz is like a white and brown ball of paper,
Taz talks by barking,
He is human,
He sleeps in the kitchen,
Or on the stairs,
Taz springs from one end of
The river to the other end,
He could win a competition,
He is wild as a cheetah,
Most of the time.

Jordan Clark (9)
Garnteg Primary School, Pontypool

Metal Dragon

'Dragon, dragon in the cave
With your star shining steel stomach,
I challenge you to a dual,'
It strolls out
Lashing and slashing,
Blue blazing eyes,
Jagged jaws,
Shooting furious flames,
It has wings of aluminium.

Aled Jenkins (10)
Garnteg Primary School, Pontypool

Cat

Tigger leaps down the stairs,
Hunting for food,
Tail wagging, lips circling around,
Tigger's enormous mouth.

Kirsty James (9)
Garnteg Primary School, Pontypool

Love

Love is as red
As your heart,
Beating back and fore
In your blood.

You feel like you are
Suddenly going to faint,
Love also wipes out everything
That you are thinking of,
Love is like a potion.

Love is like a
Silent, swooping bird,
Slowly flying across
The sky.

Derianna Thomas (8)
Garnteg Primary School, Pontypool

Buster

Buster crept through the long grass,
Stared hungrily at the little injured bird,
Buster, his long, stripy tail in the fresh air,
Licked his hungry lips and flashed his sharp, deadly claws.
Suddenly he leapt onto the bird and killed it.

Ieuan Beale (10)
Garnteg Primary School, Pontypool

Colours

Yellow is like the sun shining in the sky,
Green is like the grass blowing in the wind,
White is like the snow shining on the ground,
Blue is like the sky moving with the clouds,
Black is like the night sky sparkling like a star.

Jenna Jones (9)
Garnteg Primary School, Pontypool

Budgies

Wings like flannels, light as air,
Toes like splinters of wood,
Soft as a pillow,
They fly like butterflies,
Eyes like marbles,
Nostrils like pieces of lead,
Beaks like triangular blocks,
Heads like dandelion clocks,
Messy as a storm going to destroy town!

Rachel Gauntlett (8)
Garnteg Primary School, Pontypool

Fear

Fear is fire
Dark black
Swooping, passing
Through the grass.
Stuff burning,
Black as evil,
Fear is black
Coal, blackbirds too.

Lauren Window (8)
Garnteg Primary School, Pontypool

Sam

Sam zoomed down the tree,
Hunted for mice,
Sam crept up
And pounced onto a mouse,
Sam flashed his deadly claws,
Into the mouse and ate him.

Thomas Smith (9)
Garnteg Primary School, Pontypool

Love

Love is two swans, putting their heads together,
Making the shape of a heart,
Love is red, the same colour
As your heart beating,
Back and forward,
When you are in love,
You feel like you
Are going to suddenly
Going to faint . . .
Love is a potion
That slowly swirls
Through air.

Melissa Woollin (8)
Garnteg Primary School, Pontypool

Cat

He stretched his long stiff paws,
He arched his back,
Flopsy strolled to the door,
With his tail wagging up,
Sauntered down the street,
With a purr.

Bethan George (9)
Garnteg Primary School, Pontypool

Gerbils

Gerbils are gold,
Like a golden beach,
Sleeps like a baby,
They are really tiny, like a ring,
Never make a sound,
Their hands are like tiny diamonds.

Chloe Harvey-Delahay (9)
Garnteg Primary School, Pontypool

Colours

Red is love,
Yellow is the shining,
Sparkling sand,
Green is the shimmering,
Summer grass,
Blue is the glistening,
Gleaming sea,
Purple is a tiny flower,
Gold is your bright,
Polished earrings,
White is a fleecy,
Fluffy cloud,
Orange is a plump,
Round, juicy orange,
Pink is a rose,
Brown is a brown,
Blanket of mud.

Emma Frankum (9)
Garnteg Primary School, Pontypool

Cats

Duke pounces off the step to go in the garden
Duke stays in the grass for 10 minutes
Gets thirsty, goes to the kitchen to get some milk
He starts purring around his owner's legs.

Rhys Hatch (8)
Garnteg Primary School, Pontypool

Cat

Sam leaps off the wall to hunt mice,
He finds one, prowls, takes a leap at the mouse,
Pins it down and kills it,
Then he hides the mouse and goes to have a sip of milk.

Ian Powell (9)
Garnteg Primary School, Pontypool

Anger

Anger is like a black devil,
Coming to get you,
Making a dark sky,
Anger is a little devil biting you,
It comes over your mind,
Damaging your brain,
Anger is madness,
In your brain,
Coming to get you.

Bethan Harvey-Delahay (9)
Garnteg Primary School, Pontypool

The Bull

The bull is like a piece of darkness,
Taken from his heart to his devil.
Its heart is banging like a storm,
Knocking the door.
The bull is like something killing,
A red wedding dress on a
Woman just getting married.

Toni Dash (9)
Garnteg Primary School, Pontypool

Cat

My cat glances at a mouse,
Pouncing off the piano,
The hunt begins,
Cat soars like the wind,
Mouse is caught,
Hanging in cat's mouth.

Ellis Jones (8)
Garnteg Primary School, Pontypool

Special Days Of The Year!

1st January, New Year's Day,
Party poppers and cake all the way,
1st March, it's St David's Day,
Daffodils and leeks dressing up all day,
1st April, it's April Fool's Day,
Making jokes on people and making them pay!
6th April, it's Easter,
Chocolate eggs in the morning . . . and in the night we have pizza,
1st October, Hallowe'en night,
Where there is no light,
5th November, Bonfire Night
Where there is a lot of light,
25th December, Christmas Day,
That's the best of all!

Jordan Webb (10)
George Street Primary School, Pontypool

Through The Window

I looked through the window, what did I see?
Red primrose, white honeysuckle and pink sweetpea,
I looked through the window, what did I see?
Pretty birds, colourful butterflies and a lovely big bee.

I looked through the window, what could that be?
The wind or a storm or an owl in a tree,
I looked through the window, what did I see?
The lovely warm sun shining down on me.

I looked through the window, what could I see?
My beautiful garden that God had made for me.

Stephanie Lewis (10)
George Street Primary School, Pontypool

The Pirates From Domdiddy-Dum

Ha, ha, ha, here we come,
We are the pirates from Domdiddy-Dum,
O'er the Seven Seas,
We sail day and night,
In weather so bad, it shivers me timbers,
And my face turns white.

Ha, ha, ha, here we come,
We are the pirates from Domdiddy-Dum,
Our ship's overloaded with treasure,
Our cannons blasting into the sky,
Storms don't harm me and my crew
As we wave to passers-by.

Ha, ha, ha, we're nearly there,
Bobbing on the ocean without a care,
Through storms and sun,
Plenty of rain,
If we can get through it now,
We can do it again!

Ha, ha, ha, there we go,
Rocking in our boat, to and fro,
We're leaving the seven seas,
It's time to say goodbye,
So as we sail along,
Our cannons blast into the sky.

Hannah Haynes (11)
George Street Primary School, Pontypool

My Special Gramp

A loving Gramp, just like he is,
Caring, kind, everything you can think of.
Wherever I want to go, he takes me there,
He's got dark grey hair and brown eyes,
He loves his grandchildren a lot and he loves me.

Jamie-Leigh Passmore (9)
George Street Primary School, Pontypool

The Alien

I saw an alien
As fat as a ball
He had 7 legs
And was 3-feet tall.

He had a big head
It gave me a fright
He slept in the day
And woke up in the night.

So as I set off
I said goodbye
I got in my rocket
He started to cry.

I got to Earth
And looked at the stars
And I saw his face
That alien from Mars.

Bethan Jones (10)
George Street Primary School, Pontypool

Lonely

I'm all alone
In an empty room
Nowhere to hide.

Somehow lost
Don't know where to go
Hovering around
Can't see a way out.

Windows closed
Doors slammed shut
Tired and distressed
As I always am.

Lauren Evans (10)
George Street Primary School, Pontypool

The Snowy Christmas

T is for trees that shine in the corner,
H is for holly on the tree,
E is for excitement at Christmas time.

S is for the snowman that we all build,
N is for the carrot nose on the snowman,
O is for an orange chocolate,
W is for the winter with all the snow,
Y is for yummy chocolate money.

C is for Christmas cards that everyone has,
H is for happiness that families have,
R is for recovery time from eating all the chocolate,
I is for the ice that everyone enjoys,
S is for sitting down eating pudding,
T is for tasting chocolate off the tree,
M is for mistletoe above all the doors,
A is for all the people that we visit,
S is for the snowy Christmas we all enjoy.

Tomos Hewitt (10)
George Street Primary School, Pontypool

Looking Through The Window

Looking at the sky,
Lots of bright fire flies,
Millions of tall trees,
Got to be more than three.

I look out and see the flowers,
The way they grow, they must have powers,
At night it's really dark,
I look and see the fox and lark.

Alys Collins (10)
George Street Primary School, Pontypool

Allibis Island

Abi aims ants,
Bobby bullies bugs,
Catherine cuddles cats
        Everyone's mad on Allibis island.

Jane juggles Jona,
Nora nicks nannies,
Rosie rips rice,
        Everyone's crazy on Allibis island.

Vera's vicious vixen,
Tansey tames tea,
Lara licks lion,
        Everyone's insane on Allibis island.

But they like it just like that!

Lara Stace (10)
George Street Primary School, Pontypool

Autumn Leaves

Autumn leaves are falling,
1, 2, 3, wonder what shapes
And colours I'll see?

Falling hard, falling soft,
Right onto the ground,
I'm in the middle, they're all around.

Autumn leaves are falling,
From a high tree,
I wish I could be one of those leaves.

I wish I could be one of those leaves,
Falling to the ground and I love the way they sound.

Justine Phillips (10)
George Street Primary School, Pontypool

Hot Summer

On the blazing sunny beach,
The kids are in the sea,
All the adults on the sand,
Tanning quietly.

But now's the time I have to go,
To my lovely house,
The hours were passing really fast,
But we were travelling slow.

Shane Davis (10)
George Street Primary School, Pontypool

Why?

Why is everything as it seems?
Why does the sun shine?
Why is everyone always themselves?
Why is that pencil mine?

Why are the clouds fluffy?
Why does the grass grow?
Why is a scarecrow a scarecrow?
Why is a crow a crow?

Shona Brandon (10)
George Street Primary School, Pontypool

Best Friends

I have a best friend that is the best,
She always sticks up for me
And cheers me up if I am feeling down,
We never have an argument,
Well maybe one or two,
But then we get back together,
For ever and so on.

Samantha Carole Drew (10)
George Street Primary School, Pontypool

My Mum's Going To Kill Me

My mum is going to kill me,
I haven't done my room,
I haven't washed the dishes,
I don't know what to do.

I look at the clock,
'Oh no 5 minutes,'
What should I do?
Say I forgot, 'No, I'll tell the truth.'

Laura Cutter (10)
George Street Primary School, Pontypool

Fireworks

Fireworks are fun to see,
In colours red, blue and green,
Lots of people cheering away,
And now it's nearly the end of the day.

I'm really having a good time,
It's now only half-past nine,
Now it's time to go home to bed,
I'm tired of watching fireworks
So I'll go to sleep instead.

Emma Fellows (10)
George Street Primary School, Pontypool

Teacher

T is for the tea that teachers have at break
E is for English which they teach
A is for art that's fun, fun, fun
C is for classroom, big or small
H is for history, way in the past
E is for education, we all need
R is for resting teachers after school.

Adam J Cox (10)
George Street Primary School, Pontypool

Off To School!

You're not ill,
So why aren't you at school?
You haven't got a fever,
You haven't got mumps,
Or any funny lumps . . .

Now out of bed and off to school!

You don't look a ruin,
You don't look a wreck,
You haven't got a chill, or a pain in the neck,
You're as fit as a fiddle, as sound as a bell,
In fact I've never seen you looking so well.

Now out of bed and off to school!

Jessica Blanchard (10)
George Street Primary School, Pontypool

Eating Food

Crunch, crunch
Nibble, nibble
Crackle, crackle
Pop, pop
Goes the sound of my crisps.

Slurp, slurp
Bubble, bubble
Drip drop
Goes my pop.

Cut, cut
Scrape, scrape
Go the potatoes on my plate.

Georgia Rice (9)
George Street Primary School, Pontypool

Splodge

Splodge is my hamster, he's full of fur,
He's really cute but gets alarmed when he hears a purr.

He is always allowed out but never on his own,
He likes to run and walk about but sometimes he has a moan.

When Splodge comes out he eats a lot of fudge,
When he is eating, he will not budge.

When he is sleeping and you want him out,
You'd better be careful because he will pout.

Splodge likes to climb to the top of the cage,
And gnaw at the bars with all his rage.

His colours are light and very bright,
You can definitely see him in the dark, dark and dreary night.

He's really chubby and really cute,
But he's alarmed and really stared when I go toot, toot.

When he is running in his big yellow wheel,
He soon gets hungry and eats his meal!

Anna-Marie Bailey (10)
George Street Primary School, Pontypool

The Octopus

Deep down on the ocean floor
A monster lives ready to awake,
Creating its own earthquake,
Slowly it closes on its target,
Waiting for the night-time to attack.

It catches its opponent with its tentacle
And kills it with its toxic ink,
You'd better be careful or it'll kill you in a blink,
So don't go down to the ocean floor or
The monster will be ready!

Jack Cottrell (10)
George Street Primary School, Pontypool

Spooky House

S pooky house in the woods
P ouncing cats. Argh!
O ver the house there's a ghost
O ver the ghost, there's a cat
K nock on the door. No
Y ou knock on the door!

H ello, is anybody here?
O h wow! The cat's attacking
U nder the stairs, there's a spider
S oundless again
E very night the ghost comes out.

Emily-Jo Miller (9)
George Street Primary School, Pontypool

My Nanny Margaret

My Nanny Margaret is kind
My Nanny Margaret is helpful,
My Nanny Margaret is kind and treats me,
My Nanny Margaret is wonderful,
My Nanny Margaret is the best nan to me,
My Nanny Margaret is kind to you and me.

Charlotte Taylor (9)
George Street Primary School, Pontypool

Life's

L is for life which gives you lots of power
I is for intelligence, to be clever and to learn
F is for fear when you think something is wrong
E is for eventually, when your life ends
S is for sleeping, when you're somewhere else.

Genna Davey (10)
George Street Primary School, Pontypool

Cousin Elen

Elen is like a princess
She's very special to me
She's non-stop playful and happy
She's always there for me

Elen is always so helpful
She's never mean to me
She's one of my younger cousins
So she's depending on me!

Zoë Parker (9)
George Street Primary School, Pontypool

Joy

Joy is a room of sparkling bubbles
Delight is a pot of colourful flowers.
Contentment is a rainbow of dazzling colours,
Bliss is a bundle of freshly picked lavender,
Mirth is a pool of glistening happiness.
Ecstasy is a shining star, lighting up the world,
Pleasure is a sun in the bright blue sky,
All this is happiness.

Tansy Lydia Branscombe (9)
George Street Primary School, Pontypool

Angry Similes

As mad as a slimy slithering snake,
As crazy as a chimpanzee swinging from the highest tree.
As furious as a charging bull.
As annoyed as a zebra.
As infuriated as a lion woken from his slumber,
As cross as a leopard for not having any food
As bad-tempered as a wild ape.

Samantha Jordan (9)
George Street Primary School, Pontypool

The Great Outdoors

The great outdoors is very wide,
with lots of places to hide outside.
So no going peeping inside a tree,
you never know what there might be.

The great outdoors is very lonely
and not at all homely.
Scary places are outdoors,
and frightening animals, on all-fours.

Petrifying place is the great outdoors,
and there are certainly no laminate floorboards.
So don't you dare step outdoors -
or tigers will get you on all-fours!

Sian Kinsey (10)
George Street Primary School, Pontypool

King Of The Jungle

K ing of the jungle walks around
I ts eyes glare at you like a house cat,
N ow he's tired he has a rest for a moment,
G oing on tiptoes, very scared.

O ver a log but we made a sound,
F at eyes open wide, big as him.

T hrough the jungle he runs
H e stops and turns but doesn't turn back
E veryone is happy but the jaguar

J umps out from a cave
U nder the cave was a long green snake
N ot the jaguar nor the snake saw our feet
G orillas were being nosy but no one cared
L azy king comes back again but just lays down
E veryone was scared and didn't know what to do!

Natasha Hirons (9)
George Street Primary School, Pontypool

School Terms

School's cool, when you follow the rules,
Cool playtimes!
Jumping around,
Hot time on the field when you're bumping around,
Octopus teachers
Arms everywhere!
Oh no, you wouldn't dare!
Looking for the teacher in the staffroom.

Teachers bossing every girl and boy
Like a wobbly toy
Are you all looking at the board?
Ross is on the medical ward.
Molly sat on the milky-blue seat
Sam is waiting for his piece of meat.

Megan Jones (9)
George Street Primary School, Pontypool

My Grampa Griffiths

My Grampa is nice,
He's good at making things,
He's good at playing draughts,
And he sounds weird
When he sings.

Callum Griffiths (9)
George Street Primary School, Pontypool

National Rugby

W ales are the heroes
A nd England are the zeros
L ots of people shout and scream
E ngland are going down
S o who are the losers now?

Ross Greasley (9)
George Street Primary School, Pontypool

The Rainbow

As red as an apple on a tree
As orange as an orange in the fruit bowl
As yellow as a banana in a bunch
As green as the grass on the other side
As blue as the sky in the light
Like indigo flowers in a cup of water
Like velvety flowers you've just planted.

Sam Haynes (10)
George Street Primary School, Pontypool

Happiness

Happiness is a one pound gold coin,
Happiness tastes like a juicy melon,
Happiness smells like fresh air,
It sounds like someone is excited,
Happiness feels like you've won the lottery,
Happiness is fantastic!

Jesse Hazeldine (9)
Glyncorrwg Primary School, Port Talbot

Sadness

Sadness is as black as the night sky,
Sadness is like bitter-tasting liquorice,
Sadness is the smell of hot smoke puffing from a chimney,
Sadness is the sound of a low musical note,
Sadness is a horrible feeling inside of you.

Sophie Jones (9)
Glyncorrwg Primary School, Port Talbot

Happiness

Happiness is baby pink,
It tastes like rosy sweet berries,
It smells of tasty candyfloss
And sound of a puppy's paws patting
On the wooden floor,
Happiness is wonderful.

Danielle Down (10)
Glyncorrwg Primary School, Port Talbot

Love

Love is the colour bright red,
It tastes of delicious sweet strawberries,
It smells of an attractive ruby rose.
Love sounds like a joyful musical choir,
It feels like a new child entering the world.

Love is delightful.

Jasmin Tomlinson (10)
Glyncorrwg Primary School, Port Talbot

Anger

Anger is crimson red,
Anger tastes like extra hot chilli sauce,
Anger smells like burning fire,
It sounds like a screeching violin,
It feels like somebody being horrible to you,
Anger is being bad-tempered.

Radhika Patel (10)
Glyncorrwg Primary School, Port Talbot

Happiness

Happiness is the bright colours of the rainbow,
It tastes of strawberry gum tingling in my mouth,
It smells of the petals on a red rose,
It sounds like children playing happily on the road,
It feels like a lovely warm fur coat,
Happiness is fabulous!

Shannon Spicer (10)
Glyncorrwg Primary School, Port Talbot

Sadness

Sadness is black,
Sadness tastes like very sour vinegar,
Sadness feels like death!
Sadness sounds like a low note on a cello,
Sadness is horrid.

Shannon Harris (9)
Glyncorrwg Primary School, Port Talbot

Sadness

Sadness is dark purple,
Sadness tastes like a sour lemon,
Sadness feels like someone fitfully crying,
It sounds like a deserted graveyard,
Sadness is miserable.

Lowri Radcliffe (10)
Glyncorrwg Primary School, Port Talbot

Happiness

Happiness is relaxing lilac,
Happiness tastes like sweet juicy strawberries,
Happiness smells of red roses,
Happiness sounds like the falling of petals,
Happiness feels like the calm wind drifting across your face,
Happiness is fantastic!

Kayleigh Protheroe (9)
Glyncorrwg Primary School, Port Talbot

Jealousy

Jealousy is dark grass green,
Jealousy tastes like gone-off green cheese,
Jealousy smells of sour pickles,
Jealousy sounds like banging in your heart,
Jealousy is like someone taking over your body,
Jealousy is evil.

Christopher Howells (10)
Glyncorrwg Primary School, Port Talbot

Jealousy

Jealousy is dark emerald green,
Jealousy tastes like old mouldy cheese,
It smells of big fat pickled onions.
Jealousy sounds like thunder in your brain,
It feels like a knife thrusting inside you.
Jealousy is wicked.

Thomas Langford (10)
Glyncorrwg Primary School, Port Talbot

Happiness

Happiness is the colour of sky-blue,
Happiness tastes like pink and blue candyfloss,
Happiness smells of ripe juicy plums,
Happiness sounds like church bells ringing,
Happiness is brill.

Callum Thomas (9)
Glyncorrwg Primary School, Port Talbot

Sadness

Sadness is dark purple,
It tastes like an unpleasant tang in your mouth.
Sadness smells like death,
It sounds like people fighting and screaming at each other.
Sadness makes me feel like crying,
Sadness is pain.

Leigh Baitup (9)
Glyncorrwg Primary School, Port Talbot

Sadness

Sadness is the colour of deep black,
It tastes like bitter liquorice.
Sadness smells like rotten eggs,
It sounds like a deserted graveyard.
Sadness feels like someone stabbing you in the heart,
Sadness is horrid.

Hannah O'Gorman (10)
Glyncorrwg Primary School, Port Talbot

Love

Love is ruby-red,
It tastes like a velvety glass of smooth red wine.
Love smells like fresh red roses on Valentine's Day,
It sounds like lovebirds singing sweet songs,
It feels like somebody touching your heart,
Love is fantastic!

Alissa Bevan (10)
Glyncorrwg Primary School, Port Talbot

Happiness

Happiness is bright yellow,
It tastes like sour apple,
Happiness smells like strawberry air freshener,
It sounds like the chinking of glasses,
It feels like you're bursting with energy,
Happiness is colourful.

Adam Howells (9)
Glyncorrwg Primary School, Port Talbot

I'm Afraid Of The Dark

The dark is dark
But there's nothing to be afraid of
Except the things I imagine in my mind.
I don't like it
But I just have to accept it
And wait for daylight once again.

Kirsty King (9)
Pentrepoeth Junior School, Swansea

How To Bake The World's Best Mate

Ingredients

Pastry:
200g of caring
100 jugs of happiness
40oz of kindness
30 bowls of trustworthiness
27tsp of responsibility
2 laughters sliced finely
Friendliness grated

Toppings:
20 saucepans full of hair
2 pretty blue eyes
1 set of working arms
1 pair of helpful legs
1 smiley face
A pair of lips
A pair of good listening ears

Method:
1. Preheat oven to 180°c, gas mark 4.

2. Pour over 40oz of kindness, 100 jugs of happiness, 2 laughters chopped into half finely and friendliness grated into a bowl and stir until smooth.

3. Place the mixture into the oven and wait until half cooked, then take the mixture out of the oven and put 27tsp of responsibility, 100 jugs of happiness, 30 bowls of trustworthiness and 200g of caring onto the mixture and put back in oven for an hour.

4. When the mixture is done take it out of the oven and leave to cool. When cool place 20 saucepans full of hair, 2 pretty blue eyes, 1 pair of lips, a pair of good listening ears, 1 set of working arms, a pair of helpful legs and to top it all off a kind, smiling, happy face. That's how you bake the world's best mate.

Emily Brown (10)
Pentrepoeth Junior School, Swansea

Things, Things And Things

Babies, babies, babies
bouncing, bothering, bobbling
babies, babies, babies.

Mothers, mothers, mothers
moaning, magnificent, marvellous
mothers, mothers, mothers.

Sisters, sisters, sisters
silly, stupid, spontaneous
sisters, sisters, sisters.

Cats, cats, cats
cute, cuddly, catastrophic
cats, cats, cats.

Hamsters, hamsters, hamsters
happy, hurrying, hibernating
hamsters, hamsters, hamsters.

Teachers, teachers, teachers
telling, telling, telling
teachers, teachers, teachers.

Fish, fish, fish
funny, frolicking, fabulous
fish, fish, fish.

Puppies, puppies, puppies
puny, pet, pleasing
puppies, puppies, puppies.

Toby Parker (10)
Pentrepoeth Junior School, Swansea

Dark Is . . .

Dark is necessary, wonderful and beautiful,
It tastes like chocolate cake.
Dark is spooky, scary and silent,
It feels like a soft, furry, black bat.

Robert Costelloe (9)
Pentrepoeth Junior School, Swansea

How To Bake A Best Buddy

Ingredients:
16 jugs of intelligence
4 tablespoons of finely grated beauty
6 sprinkles of happiness
1 slice of caring
18kg of sportiness
2 arms
2 legs with knees and feet and five toes for each foot
1 body
1 head and 2 eyes and eyebrows and lips and eyelashes
2 hands and 5 fingers on each hand and lovely long fingernails
A nose with nostrils
Blonde golden hair
1 bottle of imagination
1kg of thoughtfulness
1 smile
11 sprinkles of friendliness

Put a slice of caring, sportiness and happiness in a bowl. Mix gently.
Melt 1kg of thoughtfulness in a bowl of hot water. Take off the heat.
Add 16 jugs of intelligence, stir well until smooth.
Put 1 bottle of imagination in a pan, warm gently - don't let it boil.
Make a well in centre of body parts mixture.
Pour in 1 melted smile and 4 tablespoons of beauty. Mix gently.
Don't forget the sprinkles of friendliness and a long piece of lovely
blonde golden hair.

Melinda Evans (10)
Pentrepoeth Junior School, Swansea

All About My Family

My mum is like a cuddly teddy
Because she cuddles me!
My dad is like a monster
Because he shouts at me.
My brother is like a lion
Because he growls at me.

Tyler Thomas (8)
Pentrepoeth Junior School, Swansea

Cool Poems

Lizards, lizards, lizards
lazy, long, loveable
lizards, lizards, lizards.

Chairs, chairs, chairs
comfy, cushioned, cool
chairs, chairs, chairs.

Bombs, bombs, bombs
big, bottomless, bangers
bombs, bombs, bombs.

Hamsters, hamsters, hamsters
hairy, humorous, happy
hamsters, hamsters, hamsters.

Spiders, spiders, spiders
suspicious, super, stinging
spiders, spiders, spiders.

Actors, actors, actors
active, amazing, attractive
actors, actors, actors.

Pens, pens, pens
precious, pretty, inky,
pens, pens, pens.

Beans, beans, beans
big, bulging, battered,
beans, beans, beans.

Luke Gibson (10)
Pentrepoeth Junior School, Swansea

The Mood

When I'm angry I fight,
When I'm happy I play,
When I'm sad, I go on my computer,
When I'm excited I play football.

Jack Wilcox (8)
Pentrepoeth Junior School, Swansea

I Hope

I hope . . .

I hope to be a scaffolder
Just like my dad,
I'll be in a crane building stuff,
Building work that's my dream.

I want to be . . .

I want to be a movie star,
Wow they're so lucky like Jackie Chan,
He's the best or like Arnold Schwarzenegger of 'Terminator'
Or Bruce Lee of 'The Way of the Dragon'.

I could be . . .

I could be a rugby player for Wales,
I'd be a famous martial artist
Or I could be a footballer
And play for Man United.

Jack Penhorwood (10)
Pentrepoeth Junior School, Swansea

I Wish A Lot Of Things

I wish the world was kind,
But I only wish it in my mind.
I wish the bullying would stop
So then the crying would stop.
I wish I was a horse
So I could gallop in a field.
I wish the world could see how happy I can be
So they can see silly me.
I wish I was a computer
So I could have all the technology in the world.
I wish I was as talented as a dolphin
So I could do a backflip like a dolphin too.
I wish a lot of things
And I wish they could come true.

Alisha Frater-Curtis (10)
Pentrepoeth Junior School, Swansea

If I Had A Magic Ring

If I had a magic ring
I'd wish I was a cat
So I could laze about all day long.

If I had a magic ring
I'd wish I could save all the animals
Because I love animals.

If I had a magic ring
I'd wish that it were Christmas
So I could sing merrily and have an excellent dinner.

If I had a magic ring
I'd wish I had a lot of money
So I could help the poor and be poor.

If I had a magic ring
I'd wish I were a book
So people could read me and have happy dreams.

If I had a magic ring
I'd wish I were a rose
To make the world a lovely place to live.

Caitlin Walters (10)
Pentrepoeth Junior School, Swansea

Lying In My Bed At Night

The bedroom door creaks,
Wind whistles through the window,
I see shadows on the wall,
I taste the dryness in my throat,
Quietness comes towards me,
I feel threatened inside
Until the sun comes up.

Hannah Gehrke (9)
Pentrepoeth Junior School, Swansea

I Wish . . .

I wish I could be a footballer
And play for Manchester United.

I wish it was May on a lovely summer's day
Because I would play for eternity.

I wish I was a horse
To run around all day long,
To eat loads and loads of hay
And after that go and play.

I wish I was a Martian,
To look down on Earth and watch the other Martian races.

I wish I was a stuntman
To do all magic tricks.

I wish, I wish I was a sparkling fish
With lovely rainbow scales.

Keiran Miller (10)
Pentrepoeth Junior School, Swansea

My Brother's A Right Monkey

He's messy,
He smells,
He goes to Mum and tells.

He's violent,
He's hairy,
He's really very scary.

He's crafty,
He's got brains,
He always calls me names.

But apart from that
He's alright . . .

Natasha Hilde (10)
Pentrepoeth Junior School, Swansea

I Wish I Was A Sportsman

I wish I could be an amazing
Football player
So I could be a millionaire.

I wish I could eat for Wales
So I could be big and strong.

I wish I could be amusing
To make people laugh
So I could be the funniest boy in the school.

I wish I could be an alien
So I could explore the world.

I wish I could be rich
So I could have a big house.

I wish I could be a teacher
So I could boss people around.

I wish I could be a doctor
So I could save people's lives.

Nathan Young (10)
Pentrepoeth Junior School, Swansea

My Dad Is A Gorilla . . . Argh!

He's big and hairy,
Tall and scary.
He gulps his food
And swallows it whole.
When I go to bed
I cuddle his head.
He plays and fools,
But he's really quite cool.

Tyler Ward & Yasmine Grainger (9)
Pentrepoeth Junior School, Swansea

Things I Adore

Brothers, brothers, brothers
bothering, bouncy, big
brothers, brothers, brothers.

Fish, fish, fish
fun, fearless, fantastic
fish, fish, fish.

Hamsters, hamsters, hamsters
huggable, hibernating, huge
hamsters, hamsters, hamsters.

Grampas, grampas, grampas
grumpy, generous, gentle
grampas, grampas, grampas.

Cubs, cubs, cubs
cuddly, cute, catastrophic
cubs, cubs, cubs.

Ashley Williams (10)
Pentrepoeth Junior School, Swansea

Joshua's Wish

I wish I could be a motorbiker
So I could race other people.
I wish I could be a lizard
Because I would be hot and swim every day.
I wish I could be helpful,
I would help everyone because you should respect others.
I wish I could go to the moon
So I could see the stars in space.
I wish I could go golfing,
I've got a set and it's really easy to use as long
As you keep your eye on the ball.

Joshua Bidder (10)
Pentrepoeth Junior School, Swansea

I Wish, I Wish, I Wish

I wish I was a dog
So I can chase the mailman,
Be rubbed, be fed, chase cars,
Go to the toilet anywhere,
Play with my ball,
Bark at people.

I wish I was James Bond
So I can be on TV,
Be famous, be rich, be a movie star, be a spy,
Do autographs, travel the world.

I wish I was a mechanic
So I can earn some money,
Fix stuff, be a little bit popular.

Alex Berry (10)
Pentrepoeth Junior School, Swansea

Spider Surprise

There once was a little girl,
Her name was Rosie Pearl,
She stood and watched a spider on the garden wall.
The spider jumped off with his wellies and all.
Rosie done a runner and shouted for her mother.
'The spider won't catch you, it's littler than you -
Look at his little wellies all worn through.'
Rosie had a dream, it sounded quite nice until she saw
The spider running beside her with trainers all new and clean,
Rosie woke up with a big, loud scream!

Danielle Davies (9)
Pentrepoeth Junior School, Swansea

My Birthday Wish

On my birthday I was about to blow out my candles
But I couldn't think of a wish.
Thoughts going through my head were . . .
I wish I was a dancer and a singer,
So I would be known all over the world.

I wish I was a tiny toad,
So I could hide in a garden.
(But I hope I don't get squished.)

I wish I was an elegant horse,
So I could run free and be loved.

I wish that the world would come together,
So I wouldn't be afraid of war again.

I wish I was rich,
So I could buy expensive gifts for my friends.

I wish I was a news reporter,
So I would get the latest goss.

I wish I was a model,
So I would wear the latest trends and be taller.

I wish I had a wardrobe of shoes,
So I had a dilemma every day.

But in the end I chose this wish,
I wish that all my friends and family stay happy
And well forever!

Whoosh went the candles.

Renée Bull (10)
Pentrepoeth Junior School, Swansea

How To Bake A Luscious Lass

Ingredients:
150g/5½oz luscious lips
5tbsp of lust
1tbsp of hair
100oz of kindness
3 jars of care for you
1 jar of buy you gifts
100oz of telling secrets
2tbsp of funny
11tbsp of madness
100oz of sharing
100tbsp of trust

1. Put 1tbsp of hair, 100oz of telling secrets, 3 jars of caring for you, 100oz of sharing, 2tbsp of funny in a bowl. Mix gently.

2. Melt 1tbsp of madness, 2 bottles of happiness, 100oz of kindness, 150g/5½oz of luscious lips in a bowl over hot water.

3. Take off heat. Add 5tbsp of lust, stir until smooth.

4. Put 100oz of sharing in small pan, warm gently - don't let it boil.

5. Pour in melted mix.

6. Make trustworthy by rolling 1tbsp of mixture.

7. Roll trustworthiness in sprinkles of hearts.

Now you have achieved your luscious lass.

Danielle Williams (10)
Pentrepoeth Junior School, Swansea

My Favourite Things

TVs, TVs, TVs
Terrific, terrifying, tantalising
TVs, TVs, TVs.

Games, games, games
Good, great, gripping, gruesome
Games, games, games.

Cars, cars, cars
Cracking, crazy
Cars, cars, cars.

Friends, friends, friends
Fantastic, friendly, funny
Friends, friends, friends.

Books, books, books
Brilliant, breathtaking, big
Books, books, books.

Scott Piper (11)
Pentrepoeth Junior School, Swansea

I Wish I Was The Wind

I wish I was the wind,
I could explore the world,
I would go to places that I've never been,
I would go to Italy and Belgium,
Maybe Spain and France,
I could make the trees sway and the flowers dance,
I would whistle and howl at the dead of night
And make a delightful breeze,
I would whistle a tune around the world for everyone to enjoy.

Sam Matthews (10)
Pentrepoeth Junior School, Swansea

The Flames That Find Your Wish

I wish, I wish I was a fish
With beautiful rainbow scales.
I wish I was a transformer
To transform the wars into parties.
I wish I had lots of money
To tell everyone I was funny.
I wish Pokémon was real
Because I'd like to see how it feels.
I wish I was a Jedi
To have the power of healing.
I wish some books were real
Because that would be real cool.
I wish I was half man, half dragon
Because of my love of dragons.
I wish I was an Egyptian god
Because of my love for ancient Egypt.
I wish the water was perfect
So fish and birds wouldn't die.
I wish there was no pollution
So cute little animals won't die.
I wish I could explore the universe
To see how beautiful the Earth is from space.
I wish there was no need for police
Because there is peace.
I wish there wasn't such a thing as homelessness
So there was no need for Oxfam
And people wouldn't die of starvation.
I wish I could have all these wishes
Because that's what I want to wish,
The flames have found my wish.

Joel Piper (11)
Pentrepoeth Junior School, Swansea

I Think

I think of myself upon a cloud curled,
Without a care in the world.
I think of myself flying in the sky,
Going high, oh so high.
No one could bother me not now, not ever.
I think of myself as an eagle that is fast
So I could fly around the world in a flash,
Exploring different countries.

I think of myself as the fastest man on Earth,
To tell my tale and let it last.
I think of myself as strong as an ox,
Helping people who need my help.

Christopher Fisher (10)
Pentrepoeth Junior School, Swansea

About My Family

My mum is like a rabbit
Because she is so cuddly.
My dad is like a lion
Because he's a bit nasty.
My brother is like a dog
Because he acts like one.
My big sister is like a cat
Because she loves them.
My baby sister is like a little monkey
Because she jumps everywhere in the house.
I'm like a devil
Because I am really nasty to my big sister.

Karys Turner (8)
Pentrepoeth Junior School, Swansea

My Family Zoo

My mum is a butterfly
Because she's cute and delicate.
My stepdad is a zebra
Because he's got hundreds of stripes.
My brother is a monkey
Because he's cheeky.
My sister is a rabbit
Because she likes hopping about.

Amy Raddon (8)
Pentrepoeth Junior School, Swansea

My Family Are . . .

My mum is a butterfly, she is very sweet,
She tucks me in at night and makes me go to sleep.

My dad is a dragon
Because he breaths fire like mad.

My nana is an angel because she is sweet like a fairy.
I love my family.

Gaby Taylor (8)
Pentrepoeth Junior School, Swansea

Darkness

Darkness is pitch-black,
Darkness sounds like a heavy storm,
Darkness tastes like hot chocolate,
Darkness smells like coffee,
Darkness looks like the night sky,
Darkness feels strong,
Darkness reminds me of dark coffee
And the night sky.

Jake John (10)
Pontarddulais Primary School, Swansea

Laughter

Laughter is bright yellow,
It sounds like birds singing a nice song in the morning sun.
It tastes like chocolate melting in my mouth.
It smells like lots of cake just out of the oven.
It looks like children playing in the park happily.
It feels like teddy bears.
It reminds me of mad hyenas laughing all day.

Greg Cotton (9)
Pontarddulais Primary School, Swansea

Love

Love is pink,
It sounds like doves singing a tune,
It tastes like toffee, creamy and pale,
It smells like perfume floating in the air,
It looks like a heart pounding as if she has run a mile non-stop,
It feels like a fluffy pillow,
It reminds me of a person's first kiss.

Stacey Collier (10)
Pontarddulais Primary School, Swansea

Fun

Fun is yellow,
It sounds like the flight of birds in the sky,
It tastes like cake in my mouth,
It smells like a daffodil in spring,
It looks like the sun in the sky,
It feels like a warm day in the midst of summer.

Daniel Jones (10)
Pontarddulais Primary School, Swansea

Darkness

Darkness is black like a witch.
It's like a dark hole that never ends,
It just goes on and on.
It sounds like a wolf howling on a frosty
Hill in front of a misty moon.
It tastes like hot, sizzling acid
Bubbling up from my mouth.
It looks like a volcano ready
To erupt at any moment.
It looks like a devil taking people's
Souls in the middle of the night.
It feels like someone just punched
Me with a heavy round brick covered in blood.
It reminds me of somebody on their own
In a big empty room in complete darkness.

Steffan Williams (10)
Pontarddulais Primary School, Swansea

Love

Love is pink,
It sounds like doves
In the tree cooing together,
It tastes like marshmallows
Melting in my mouth,
It smells like melting chocolate
Bubbling in a pan,
It looks like a hare,
It feels soft and warm,
It reminds me of my family.

James Beynon (10)
Pontarddulais Primary School, Swansea

Laughter

Laughter is orange,
It sounds like a gurgling stream,
It tastes like exploding sherbet,
It smells like melting chocolate
Bubbling in a pot,
It looks like children playing in the schoolyard,
It feels like excitement,
It reminds me of a holiday in the sun.

Jordan Thomas (10)
Pontarddulais Primary School, Swansea

Anger

Anger is red,
It sounds like a big, loud rumble,
It tastes like super duper sour bomb sweets,
It smells like rotting fish with smelly scales
That have lost their colour,
It looks like a scary red devil,
It feels hot and sweaty,
It reminds me of friends being horrid.

Tom Cowley (10)
Pontarddulais Primary School, Swansea

Love

Love is pink like roses.
It feels like my heart is beating so fast that I can hardly breathe.
It tastes like juicy, luscious strawberries trickling down my throat.
It looks like a crystal pink sunset filling the sky.
It smells like fresh, red roses swaying in the breeze.
It sounds like a glistening ocean hitting the crystal rocks.
It reminds me of a glistening diamond ring put on someone's finger.

Lowri Davies (9)
Pontarddulais Primary School, Swansea

Sadness

The colour of sadness is yellow daisies.
Sadness tastes like a burning flame of fire in your mouth,
Just about to stain your tongue.
It sounds like a lone saxophone playing
In the dead of night.
It smells like coffin dust just been swept up off the coffin.
It reminds me of a bird just dying
And having its last chance
Of flapping its beautiful wings.

Rebecca Aubrey (10)
Pontarddulais Primary School, Swansea

Fun

Fun is yellow.
It sounds like mermaids singing in the ocean.
It tastes like a rainbow Slush Puppy.
It smells like a portion of pink, red and white roses.
It looks like cats and dogs playing with each other.
It feels like a polar bear and its cubs
Falling to sleep with you.
It reminds me of dancing in a disco at a wedding.

Kurt Thomas (10)
Pontarddulais Primary School, Swansea

Love

Love is a calm, soft pink,
Love sounds like a new baby chick chirping,
Love tastes like freshly picked strawberries,
Love smells like a newborn baby,
Love looks like the sun fading away,
It feels warm and gentle,
It reminds me of my family and friends.

Cody-Lea Gross (10)
Pontarddulais Primary School, Swansea

Fun

Yellow is the colour of fun
Where the sun shines and rabbits are hopping everywhere.
Fun sounds like people enjoying themselves
On holiday in the sun outside, or in the pool.
Fun tastes like a block of white chocolate
Melting in my mouth and sliding down my throat.
Fun smells like a huge field of buttercups.
Fun looks like bunnies jumping in the garden with their mother.
Fun feels like having a ball with all your friends all night long.
Fun reminds me of friends and family on special occasions.

Rebecca Hopkins (9)
Pontarddulais Primary School, Swansea

Fun

Yellow is the colour of fun.
Fun sounds like birds singing in the tree.
Fun tastes like a big bubble of laughter.
Fun smells like happiness in the air.
Fun looks like a big colourful rainbow
Stretched across the sky.
Fun feels like playing all day long.
Fun reminds me of playing on the grass with my dad.

Michael Grey (9)
Pontarddulais Primary School, Swansea

Fun

Fun is blue.
It sounds like people screaming with joy.
It tastes like melting chocolate on my tongue.
It smells like Dairy Milk.
It looks like a puppy dog.
It feels like summertime.
It reminds me of children playing in the park.

Tom Hesford (10)
Pontarddulais Primary School, Swansea

Hunger

Hunger is brown.
It sounds like grumbling deep down in your stomach.
It tastes like sand that's been in your mouth for days.
It smells like a river that has dried up
And has been like that for years.
It looks like a dark, empty hole under miles of desert
With not even a drip of water.
It feels like the vibrations of a drum booming inside you.
It reminds me of people without food or water.

Hannah Duncan (10)
Pontarddulais Primary School, Swansea

Love

Love is a pinky-rose colour.
It sounds like a newborn chick chirping in the midday sun.
It tastes like sweet candy fresh from the sweet shop
Popping in your mouth.
It smells like fresh popcorn being made in the oven.
It looks like roses swaying in the morning breeze.
It feels like happiness flowing everywhere.
It reminds me of new doves having a flying lesson.

Liam Chambers (10)
Pontarddulais Primary School, Swansea

Love

Love is a peaceful carnation, perky pink.
Love sounds like a harp playing on a cold and snowy mountain.
Love tastes like a sweet, pink, freshly picked raspberry.
Love smells like a peaceful garden full of roses.
Love looks like two deadly in love people
Getting married in a church.
Love feels like someone running through a field full of roses.
Love reminds me of someone reading in their bed.

Francesca Rix (10)
Pontarddulais Primary School, Swansea

Fun

Fun is turquoise.
It sounds like people splashing
On a hot summer's day
In a big, deep pool.
It tastes like succulent mint
Choc chip ice cream.
It smells like tulips on
Green, green grass in the park.
It feels as if you're going to burst open
Because you're so excited.
Looks like swimming with dolphins
In the blue and green sea.
It reminds me of the
Happiest day in my life.

Kayleigh Howells (10)
Pontarddulais Primary School, Swansea

Darkness!

Darkness is black as space.
It is like a black, gargantuan, bottomless hole
Full of knives plunging in your back
With iron blades whipping your heart.
It sounds like a whale crying into the open sea.
It tastes like toxic gas floating down my throat.
It smells like burning firewood burning, flaming through the night.
It looks like an empty space filling with darkness.
It feels like somebody whipping you with chains.
It reminds me of the universe, empty but sad.

Thomas Evans (10)
Pontarddulais Primary School, Swansea

Love

Love is red, like juicy strawberries
Just picked out of a colourful and beautiful garden.
It looks like the yellow baby chicks that were hatched yesterday.
Smells like the ruby roses and feels
Like the wind on a summer's day.
It tastes like chocolate melting in your mouth
And trickling down your throat.
Love reminds me of happiness and nature,
And my friends.

Charlotte Davies (10)
Pontarddulais Primary School, Swansea

Love

The colour of love is a bright red,
Red as the rosiest cheek in the world.
It sounds like sweet music playing in the breeze.
It tastes like luscious, sweet strawberries with cream.
It smells like sweet passionfruit.
It looks like people dancing in the precious moonlight.
It feels like a happy, tingling, warm feeling.
It reminds me of two people who love each other.

Ashley Mbofana (10)
Pontarddulais Primary School, Swansea

Fun

Fun is happiness, rosy-red happiness.
It smells of luscious red roses in the garden.
It tastes of bubbling hot, melted chocolate in your mouth.
It feels like a slow breeze swooping through the air.
It looks like a bottle of champagne bursting open.
Fun reminds me of running along boiling hot sand
And jumping in the sea.
Fun sounds like sherbet popping in your mouth.

Natasha Harris (10)
Pontarddulais Primary School, Swansea

Love

Red is a colour of love,
Like bright roses gleaming in the sunshine.
It sounds like a harp playing in the distance above.
Love tastes like a juicy, red strawberry
And the seeds are crackling in my mouth.
Love smells like a field full of bright flowers.
Love looks like a red heart
Gleaming in my eyes.
Love feels like a big, fluffy teddy bear
Cuddled in my arms.
Love reminds me of my
Lovely family and friends.

Louise Eynon (9)
Pontarddulais Primary School, Swansea

Darkness

Darkness is black, it is like the night sky.
It sounds like a black wolf howling
At the silver, glowing, midnight moon.
It tastes like a rotten egg oozing down your throat.
It smells like a rotten dump site of toxic waste.
It looks like a damp snake pit
With a million snakes inside.
It feels like a cold hand touching your shoulder
And dragging you away.
It reminds you of a dark twister spinning away.

Amy Thomas (10)
Pontarddulais Primary School, Swansea

Silence

Silence is elegant and white
Like snow in the cold winter season.
It sounds really calm and peaceful,
Like the water lying still by itself
On the blue sea.
It tastes like gorgeous, soft,
Whipped cream on a hot cappuccino.
The smell of it is like air, floating up
In the big blue sky.
It looks like glowing, glittering powder
All around you.
It feels like delicate tissue paper
Wiping your cheek.
It reminds me of laying on a sunny beach
Relaxing by myself.

Jodie Rogers (10)
Pontarddulais Primary School, Swansea

Anger

Anger is hot, burning, flaming, peppery, red.
Anger is like a bubbling, burning, flaming
Hot volcano bursting inside of me.
Anger sounds like a really high-pitched scream.
Anger tastes like a flaming, burning, hot
Slice of pepperoni pizza.
Anger smells like super smelly piece of pineapple pizza.
Anger looks like a devil sucking someone's soul out.
Anger feels like a beast leaping out of my heart.
Anger reminds me of someone dying a very,
Very, very, very, very slow and painful death.

James Evans (10)
Pontarddulais Primary School, Swansea

Hate

Hate is a fiery red colour.
It is like being stabbed a
Million times in the back
With a boiling hot skewer.
Hate sounds like a gigantic
Volcano ready to erupt.
It tastes like toxic poison
Just come out of a furnace.
Hate smells like burning
A million forests.
It looks like a red-horned devil
Is shooting missiles through the sky.
Hate feels like hatred
Rushing through your body.
It reminds me of losing
The only thing I ever wanted.

Sam Thomas (10)
Pontarddulais Primary School, Swansea

Fun!

Fun is yellow.
It sounds like laughter.
It tastes like chips and curry,
All spicy in my mouth.
It smells like yellow roses,
Growing in my garden.
It looks like children playing together.
It feels like a nice day.
It reminds me of my birthday party
With all my friends.

Jake Thomas (11)
Pontarddulais Primary School, Swansea

Anger

Anger is red.
It sounds like steam pouring from a kettle.
It tastes like boiling water burning my tongue.
It smells like filthy socks, all sweaty and smelly.
It looks like a storm, thunder and lightning
Flashing across the sky.
It feels hot and sweaty and uncomfortable.
It remind me of friends being nasty and unfriendly.

Sam Bevan (10)
Pontarddulais Primary School, Swansea

Fun

Fun is yellow.
It sounds like birds singing, children singing.
It tastes of sherbet popping in my mouth.
It smells like chocolate.
It looks like a party.
It is fun.
It feels like happiness running through my body.
It reminds me of a party.

Thomas Lloyd (10)
Pontarddulais Primary School, Swansea

Love

Pink is the colour of love.
It sounds like newborn chicks chirping in springtime.
Bright, juicy, red, luscious, soft strawberries tingle down my throat.
It smells like fresh daisies as I lower my face down into a bouquet.
It looks like two white doves flying into the sunset.
It feels as if you've just won the lottery.
It reminds me of flowers blooming in the hot summertime.

Laura-May James (10)
Pontarddulais Primary School, Swansea

Fun

Fun is yellow.
It sounds like laughter.
It tastes like chocolate.
It smells like caramel.
It looks like a happy dog
Enjoying a run around in the park.
It feels like soft fur, warm to my touch.
It reminds me of my brother's birthday.

Liam Howells (10)
Pontarddulais Primary School, Swansea

Laughter

Laughter is a fun, bubbly orange.
It sounds like a dolphin skipping in and out of waves.
It tastes like chocolate melting on your tongue.
It smells like a lavender flower opening up to the sunrays.
Laughter looks like bubbles exploding in the air.
It feels like running down a hill on a nice, dry, sunny day.
Laughter reminds me of being with my friends.

Thomas Brauner (10)
Pontarddulais Primary School, Swansea

Silence

Silence is like white doves and snow, floating in the sky.
It sounds like the ocean at night.
It tastes like whipped cream trickling down my throat.
It smells like floating air in the body.
It looks like rain dripping down from the sky.
It feels like soft tissue paper wiping my skin.
Silence reminds me of relaxing on my bed, reading,
While the world's asleep.

Hannah Jones (10)
Pontarddulais Primary School, Swansea

Love

Love is red like juicy, sweet, luscious strawberries.
It sounds like doves singing in springtime.
It tastes like a delicious Sunday dinner.
It smells like perfume on a hot summer's day.
It looks like a bunch of flowers,
With birds singing happily
On the branch of a tree.
It feels like a tingly feeling
Running through your body.
It reminds me of weddings,
With people laughing and dancing *happily!*

Sophie Burgess (11)
Pontarddulais Primary School, Swansea

Happiness

Happiness is white like snow in the wintertime.
It sounds like Mum's singing in the bath.
It tastes like ice water.
It smells like Mum's beautiful perfume.
It looks like my mum's dark, shiny hair.
It feels like the cuddle Mum gives me before bedtime.
Happiness reminds me of my mum.

Callum Thomas (7)
Pontarddulais Primary School, Swansea

Happiness

Happiness is white fluffy clouds floating by on a sunny summer's day.
Happiness sounds like children laughing.
Happiness tastes like ice water.
Happiness looks like children playing
Happiness feels like a bright colour.
Happiness reminds me of my dad.

Shaun Harris (7)
Pontarddulais Primary School, Swansea

Anger

Anger is a dark red colour.
It sounds like a kettle whistling with all its might.
It tastes like hot chocolate that's just been poured over
                              Rice Crispie cakes.
It smells like smoke from a fire.
It looks like a hurricane.
It feels like boiling hot lava pouring from a volcano.
It reminds me of having my appendix removed!

Reiner Wolf (10)
Pontarddulais Primary School, Swansea

Anger

Anger is red like a devil, like fire.
Anger sounds like tearing and crashing.
Anger tastes like rotten eggs.
Anger smells like the drains in the summer heat.
Anger looks like a devil.
Anger feels like barbed wire.
Anger reminds me of a devil's tail,
All sharp and spiky.

Trystan Bateman (7)
Pontarddulais Primary School, Swansea

Sadness

Sadness is black like a black cloud in a rainy sky.
Sadness sounds like rain on a windowpane.
Sadness tastes like your food gone cold.
Sadness smells like a cold, damp night.
Sadness looks like a very dark cloud.
Sadness feels dreadful.
Sadness reminds me of a big, bad storm.

Mathew Thomas (7)
Pontarddulais Primary School, Swansea

Sadness

Sadness is black like a black cloud.
Sadness is like thunder and lightning.
Sadness sounds like a storm raging.
Sadness tastes like gone-off food.
Sadness smells like rotten eggs.
Sadness looks like a rain cloud.
Sadness feels like nobody's my friend.
Sadness reminds me of my grandma.

Myles Oliver Santino Davies (7)
Pontarddulais Primary School, Swansea

Fear

Fear is black like a big, black cave.
It sounds really scary.
Fear tastes like really thick blood.
Fear smells like thick smoke.
Fear looks like a dog running.
Fear feels like you want to hide.
Fear reminds me of my sister on the computer.

Chloe Scott (7)
Pontarddulais Primary School, Swansea

Joy

Joy is bright yellow,
Like sweet sugar and autumn days.
It sounds like the wind blowing.
It tastes like strawberries.
It smells like perfume.
It looks like the sunset.
It feels smooth.
Joy reminds me of people playing perfectly.

Janine Stephenson (8)
Pontarddulais Primary School, Swansea

Sadness

Sadness is blue like icy water.
Sadness sounds like a dog howling in pain.
Sadness tastes like food that's gone cold.
Sadness smells like damp clothes.
Sadness looks like wallpaper hanging off the wall.
Sadness feels like the softness of rotten fruit.
Sadness reminds me of puppies with no home.

Ieuan Derrick (8)
Pontarddulais Primary School, Swansea

Fear

Fear is brown, like the cupboards in my kitchen.
Fear sounds like a lion with bright eyes, roaring.
Fear tastes like the spicy peanuts I have on my food.
Fear smells like brown apples which are rotten.
Fear looks like monsters creeping up on you.
Fear feels like when you're cold and shivery.
Fear reminds me of a black night-time sky.

Sophie Elizabeth Thomas (7)
Pontarddulais Primary School, Swansea

Love

Love is light pink, like sweet, beautiful candyfloss.
Love sounds like flowing music.
Love tastes like sweet, sugary jam.
Love smells like sweet flowers.
Love looks like sweet cuddles and kisses.
Love feels like a soft, gentle touch.
Love reminds me of sweet, smooth things.

Sara-Leah Mullen (8)
Pontarddulais Primary School, Swansea

Love

Love is the colour of bright, luscious red roses.
It sounds like the calm blue ocean
Coming over the sandy, shimmering beach.
It tastes like chopped up, juicy red strawberries
Trickling down my throat.
It smells like the beautiful breezy air coming towards you.
It looks like the sparkling sun
Shining down on the flowery green hills.
It feels like you're wrapped up
In a hot, warm, purple, glamorous quilt.
It reminds me of weddings, of happiness and joy.
Elinor Eynon (9)
Pontarddulais Primary School, Swansea

Anger

Anger is red.
It feels unhappy.
It tastes like sick.
It smells like dog food.
It looks like a big bad wolf.
It feels sharp and prickly.
It reminds me of a lion roaring.
Shannon Davies (7)
Pontarddulais Primary School, Swansea

Happiness

Happiness is yellow, like the sun shining brightly.
It sounds like the birds singing.
It tastes like fresh strawberries and cream.
It smells like a packet of cola bottle sweets.
It looks like a kitten playing with a toy mouse.
It feels like a new quilt, all soft and fluffy.
Happiness reminds me of my holiday in Spain.
Chloe Rees (7)
Pontarddulais Primary School, Swansea

Love

Love is a beautiful dark red rose
Which sounds like doves singing in the trees.
To me it tastes like sugary, sweet
Juicy strawberries and smells
Like fresh summer honey.
It looks like two roses standing
Alone in a beautiful garden and
Feels like springs bouncing in my body.
It reminds me of laughter and hot sunny days.

Chloe Stephenson (10)
Pontarddulais Primary School, Swansea

Ghosts Are Spooky

G hosts are leaping over dead bodies,
H aunted spirits seek the mansion,
O h my God! What was that?
S eek the mansion and you'll become one of them!
T orturing, bloodthirsty vampires sucking blood,
S keletons diving into baths of blood.

A re you scared yet?
R unning skeletons whose legs come off.
E mbarrassed zombies who lost their clothes.

S tupendously tall towers,
P oof - here come the vampires,
O oooh! Ghosts are lurking round the corner.
O h my gosh, what was that?
K illing vampires trying to kill me!
Y elling as I zoom down the corridor, 'Argh!'

Lauran Allford (10)
St Mary's CW Primary School, Brynmawr

Meerkat

He has small, hairy toes,
And so does his family and his foes.
His hair is like string stuck on with glue,
He stands on two legs like all of them do.
Standing up on their two back legs,
Their two paws together as if to beg.
Their paws are quite small and look like their feet.
They use their paws to help them eat.
Their tails are long and point at the end,
If you look at their tails, they straighten and bend.
Their heads are small with big, beady eyes,
Some of them look like they're spies.

I like these animals, I like them a lot.
I'd like to become one, I'd like that a lot!

Beth Lewis (10)
St Mary's CW Primary School, Brynmawr

My Wish Poem

I would like . . .

A sack full of happiness,
A dish full of smiles,
A cup full of friendship,
A packet full of love,
A box full of peace,
A bottle full of kindness,
A bag full of surprises,
A glass full of helpfulness.

Laurie Carey (7)
St Mary's CW Primary School, Brynmawr

White

Her feet are spiky, like a mountain of thorns.
Her legs are fat!
Her round, curvy body is enormous.
She's furry and white all around.
Her ears are like half circles
And her face is like a triangle.
Her eyes are wide open for the celebration.
Her nose is long and curvy on the end.
Her mouth is large and full of danger
That could kill you in minutes.
Now it's happening, her baby cub is born.
Polar bear puts her new cub on her back.

Holly Thomas
St Mary's CW Primary School, Brynmawr

My Wish Poem

I would like . . .

A packet full of friendship,
A house full of happy families,
A sack full of kindness,
A bag full of love,
A dish full of happiness,
A plate full of smiles,
A box full of surprises,
A bottle full of laughter,
And a school full of happy children.

Callum Kershaw
St Mary's CW Primary School, Brynmawr

The Tiger

The claws on the tiger are pointed and sharp,
Legs are furry and fluffy like the fur on a monkey.
Body is big and orange, white and black,
Head and face are like a football.
Ears are like big, pointed, fluffy things.
Whiskers are like sticks, but bendy and white.
Eyes are like rolling marbles, staring at you
When he is going to kill you.
Suddenly he's off for the chase.
He is pouncing up and down.
When he is ready, he'll jump for his prey and *bang!*
He's ripping into him and it falls to the floor in a quick motion
And it's dying in pain and he's killed his prey.

Jack James
St Mary's CW Primary School, Brynmawr

My Wish Poem

I would like . . .

A sack full of love,
A bag full of happiness,
A box full of wealth,
A plate full of laughter,
A bottle full of friendship,
A bed full of rest,
And a case full of gold.

Bethan Jenkins (8)
St Mary's CW Primary School, Brynmawr

A Sunny Morning

Their paws are like claws,
That make you faint like poison.
They have dark red eyes that make you smile.
The cubs grow big and strong.
They have legs that look like plain bones
Like their claws.
The cubs are really nasty and
They eat fresh meat from their prey.
They chase their prey like mad.
They run faster than leopards,
They are fast like the wind.
Their whiskers are like strings.
They eat elephants and more.
What is it? A cheetah.

Zoe Pope (10)
St Mary's CW Primary School, Brynmawr

My Wish Poem

I would like . . .

A glass full of happiness,
A bowl full of smiles,
A sack full of love,
A bottle full of laughter,
A plate full of peace,
A cracker full of surprises,
A bag full of wealth,
A mug full of beauty.

Molly Tucker (7)
St Mary's CW Primary School, Brynmawr

The Snowy Day

He has soft fur like a pillow.
He has sharp claws.
He has straight legs.
All you can see is white fur.
He lies on his back.
He has sparkling eyes,
He also has pointy ears
And his eyes are pitch-black.
His ears are soft and warm.
He loves the snow and he lies on it.
He walks on four legs.
He eats fish.
Sometimes he is really noisy.
Sometimes he sleeps all day.
Do you know what he is? A polar bear.

Corienne Madden (10)
St Mary's CW Primary School, Brynmawr

My Wish Poem

I would like . . .

A sack full of smiles,
A room full of happiness,
A bottle full of surprises,
A plate full of love,
A packet full of friendship,
A house full of peace,
A cracker full of wealth,
And a school full of happy children.

Rhys Cook (7)
St Mary's CW Primary School, Brynmawr

Vampires Suck Blood

V ampires have scary fangs
A wake at night, sleep by day
M ust hide at night,
P eeking round the corner at their supper
I nside their coffins they sleep.
R unning away from anyone who sees them,
E xtremely hungry for blood,
S peeding to their coffins at dawn.

S ucking blood to stop their thirst,
U gly vampires with boils and zits,
C ourage is what I need
K illing people with their fangs.

B lood is what they need
L icking the blood from people's necks
O h no, it's after me!
O pening its mouth it shouts, 'Yum-yum!'
D aytime, you never see them!

Nia Follis (9)
St Mary's CW Primary School, Brynmawr

The Elephants

Their feet look like huge balls of soft dough,
They hit the hard, solid floor one after the other.
Smooth, leathery skin gets dirty from the mud.
Meanwhile, their tusks stick out like massive fangs.
Patiently, slowly, they travel with their families to find any sign of water.
Slowly, as the sun goes down, it's time for them to move again,
                              always searching.

Hâf Philpotts-Davies (10)
St Mary's CW Primary School, Brynmawr

Haunted Holiday

H aunted holiday,
A skeleton in the hotel,
U nusual noises echo at midnight,
N o clean water, the ghosts drink it all,
T he ghosts steal a cup of tea,
E ditor from the newspaper is flying round the room,
D ead people found in their beds at night.

H aunted holiday,
O range blood going down the stairs,
L ittle men are trying to kill the skeletons,
I don't like the hotel, it is very smelly.
D avid, my brother, is flying round the room,
A nd my brother Gareth is hiding in the wardrobe.
Y owling ghosts trying to kill the manager.
    Why did you pick this hotel?

Ben Lewis (9)
St Mary's CW Primary School, Brynmawr

My Wish Poem

I would like . . .

A box full of happiness,
A dish full of generosity,
A sack full of friendship,
A cup full of smiles,
A cracker full of surprises,
A mug full of laughter.

Matthew Lewis-Richards (7)
St Mary's CW Primary School, Brynmawr

The Rabbit

Little sharp claws, very bold,
Hairy and furry, never cold.
Little short legs, hopping up and down,
Even if you're quiet, you won't hear a sound.
Small little body, ever so neat,
And if you see its small tail,
It's oh, so sweet.
Cute little face, from left to right,
Glittery eyes, perfect sight.
Button nose, floppy ears,
Fox is her fear.

Taylor James (10)
St Mary's CW Primary School, Brynmawr

Hallowe'en

H aunted mansions rule the world!
A llowing skeletons to murder,
L urking skeletons knocking on doors,
L ovely blood puddles!
O h no, here they come,
W olves with blood dripping from their teeth,
E veryone run before they have fun,
E veryone run! Everyone!
N ever come back! Never come back!

Brooke Lewis-Richards (10)
St Mary's CW Primary School, Brynmawr

Our School Is Cool

My school is cool,
Mr Smith's no fool.
Mr Cole's got soul,
Mrs Chaplin's a-rappin'.
Mrs Morgan plays the organ,
Mrs Thomas likes her commas,
Miss Rees phones the police
About the vandals in our school,
Miss Mallet likes Hamlet,
Miss Stevens likes evens,
Miss Lewis does the music,
Mrs Wright's giant
Gives us a fright,
Mr Forbes swings like doors.

Lauren Cook (9)
St Mary's CW Primary School, Brynmawr

Spooky, Scary

S cary skeletons saying, 'Go away'
P opping up heads from the graves,
O pening doors and windows,
O ver the night spirits floating around,
K illing ghouls are around,
Y ou've got to go!

S cary ghouls scare me
C reaking stairs frighten me
A aargh! Ghosts, ghouls and spirits
R ound and round the windmill goes until a ghost pops out!
Y ou, you go away. *No, no, no.*

Connor Edwards
St Mary's CW Primary School, Brynmawr

Red Arrows

Oh I'd like to fly an Arrow,
It would be such fun,
To fly around in the snow
And in the sun.
Oh I want to fly an Arrow,
Oh a Red Arrow would be fun,
To fly around over,
The wind and the sun.
Oh I'd like to fly an Arrow,
Oh wouldn't it be fun to watch,
An arrow shine in the sun?
Oh I would like to fly an Arrow,
Oh it would be so much fun,
But I've only got a model
And the model's not done!

Gawain Pope (9)
St Mary's CW Primary School, Brynmawr

Skeletons

S cary skeletons spook the night,
K ind of give you a nasty fright,
E nvious enemies end the day,
L ions prowl in the middle of May.
E very skeleton likes their bed.
T all, bloodthirsty creatures dribble and drool,
O range beards left in the pool,
N asty newts feel quite sore,
S piderwebs hang by the door.

Hannah Carey (9)
St Mary's CW Primary School, Brynmawr

Have A Nice Fright!

H ave a good scare
A n evil evening
V ampires hiding under the bed
E lectric has failed!

A ghost!

N ot again!
I' m coming to get you
C oaches arriving at the stroke of midnight
E ven our guard dog is scared!

F angs sink into the night
R unning up and down the stairs
I can't see Dad's reflection
G hosts out looking for ghoul-friends
H owling at the moon
T apping noises on the roof!

Chloe Jones
St Mary's CW Primary School, Brynmawr

The Chasing Game

The little cutie cat
Was tempted to chase a rat,
But then the cat found something
Better than that, a hat, a very feathery hat.
Cat pouncing through the long grass by and by
The hat blows, oopsie daisy, there it goes
And lands in a nest of crows, with very colourful bows!
The little cutie cat climbed up the tree and
Oh no! The cat got stung by a bee
And flew out of the tree as fast as could be!

Elys Philpotts-Davies (10)
St Mary's CW Primary School, Brynmawr

Spooky Mansion

S cary ghosts going round
P eople hanging by the neck
O pposite the mirror I see a face
O n the landing I hear a creepy sound
K eep out, we're about
Y ou are trapped

M onster mummies killing you
A gainst the law
N othing's here, I'm scared
S cary skeletons
I can see you
O ooh!
N o! Go away!

Della Jenkins (9)
St Mary's CW Primary School, Brynmawr

Year 5 Classroom

In Year 5 classroom
The books are in the trays,
The work is so, so cool,
You want to miss the plays!

In Year 5 classroom
The teachers are cool dudes,
They help you all the way,
So show good attitude.

In Year 5 classroom
You'll hear the kids shout,
'This place is too cool, so
No one let us out!'

Lauren Elias (9)
St Mary's CW Primary School, Brynmawr

Skeletons Are Bony

S keletons are spooky
K ind? You must be joking!
E veryone is terrified
L isten to them snapping
E veryone, you'd better run!
T onight they will come out
O n the stairs they will run, without a doubt
N ever see them in the day
S o you'll be shouting, haaaaa!

A aah!
R rrrun!
E eeek!

B elieve me, now I'm really scared
O h my gosh, what was that?
N ear the back door creaks, everyone screams and screeches
Y elling as I run away!

Rebecca Pritchard
St Mary's CW Primary School, Brynmawr

Ghosts Hunt

G o away you horrible ghost. Oh no, it's Mr Cole!
H ow could it be my teacher? It is a ghost.
O h, so what, just leave him, get along.
S top Mr Cole, you are arrested for attempted murder.
T he souls floating round howling at a mansion.
S keletons hanging, blood on the walls, stay away or I'll haunt you all!

H unt, hunt, hunt, Mr Cole, he's my teacher, oh no!
U ntil the sunset comes down, he will be a teacher.
N ight has come and Emily is scared of her uncle.
T he sun has risen, he's all gone. Yay, celebration!

Danielle Crawford
St Mary's CW Primary School, Brynmawr

Scary Vampires And Witches' Holiday

S pirits scream,
C ells lock you in,
A liens invade
R hinos kill you
Y ou fall dead

V ampires bite your bloody necks
A spaceship hits Earth
M orons get you
P irates make you walk the plank
I rresponsible spooks
R eading master gets you
E nemies die
S inking Titanic

A nts grow
N ormans raid
D evils get you

W itches drown you in their potion
I ndians hang you
T error hits Earth
C omets hit Mars
H aunted mansion scares you to death
E eeeee!
S adly you die

H ell breaks open
O ctopus grabs you
L adies turn mad
I llness and disease hit you
D inosaurs chase you
A nimals die
Y owling werewolf
S ouls scared. Run!

Matthew Collier (9)
St Mary's CW Primary School, Brynmawr

The Hunter

His claws remain still until he can pounce.
He's like a flashing light in the forest.

His stripes are blurred while in the chase,
While his prey is speedily escaping.

His neck is stretched,
Trying to get closer to his victim.

His ears are listening to the rustling bushes,
He is concentrating on his prey.

His eyes are staring,
Like two deadly black marbles.

His nose can smell the scent of the animal,
He cannot wait to pounce.

His grin becomes wider,
He is catching up with his prey.

Then he clamps onto his prey . . .
The tiger will live another day.

Adrienne Cox
St Mary's CW Primary School, Brynmawr

Vampires

V ampires biting on Hallowe'en
A nxious devils lurking about
M any witches flying about, casting spells
P eople turning red and yellow, turning into frogs
I nside the coffin
R ed vampires sneaking up and going, *'Boo!'*
E verybody sinking in quicksand
S ee you soon - 'Argh!'

Nina Pickering (9)
St Mary's CW Primary School, Brynmawr

The Beano Is The Best

The Beano is the best,
The Dandy is the worst,
I love the Beano so much,
My brain is going to burst!

The Beano is the best,
There's Dennis and Roger,
Minnie the Minx and Ballboy,
And Dodge Cat a Dodger.

The Beano is the best,
The Softies are the worst,
The Menaces are my favourites,
So I think they come first!

The Beano is the best,
I see it on telly,
There's Dennis the Menace and Gnasher,
With sweets in their bellies!

Regine Tse (9)
St Mary's CW Primary School, Brynmawr

Ghosts Haunt

G hosts are haunting the mansion and dead bodies
H a, ha, ha, we are alive!
O h no, run . . .
S tormy weather, ghosts come out
T rees swinging back and fore
S cary vampires haunt the mansion with the ghosts.

H allowe'en seeks us as we run from ghouls
A fter tonight I'm moving from town
U gly spirits with boils and burns
N aughty spirits pulling faces
T ouching ghosts stealing clothes.

Meghan Bolter
St Mary's CW Primary School, Brynmawr

Animals

Bats and rats are like each other,
They both come out at night.
When you have gone to bed,
They go left and right.

Tigers and lions run about,
Chasing all their prey,
If they see you try to catch them,
They will make you run away.

Frogs, lizards and crocodiles,
Are all reptiles.
When the sky is nice and sunny,
You might see one, they are very funny.

But the animals I like most
Are those duck-billed platypuses
And little black bunnies.

Danielle Cox
St Mary's CW Primary School, Brynmawr

Monkeys

The monkeys race to get together,
They hurry up the trees when they see humans.
They scatter when they see food.
They act the same as humans.
They climb the highest trees around,
They race to the highest branch.
Their ears look like antelopes'.
Their fur sticks up like they are in shock.
Their mouths are thin and timid.
They climb up a tree and sit and stare.

Lewis Cable
St Mary's CW Primary School, Brynmawr

There Are Many Animals In The World

There are many animals in the world,
And one I like is the big elephant with tusks
Which have a spike.
There are many animals in the world,
And best by far is the parrot that talks
In the forest, he's such a star.
There are many animals in the world,
And the one I hate is the rattle
Of the frightening rattlesnake.
There are many animals in the world,
And the one I'm not sure about
Is the lion with a roar that is like thunder
That is loud.

Antonia Gullick (8)
St Mary's CW Primary School, Brynmawr

The Bengal Tiger

B engal tigers have powerful hind legs,
E nding with immense paws,
N o animal can beat the Bengal tiger,
G iant paws can knock over prey with one blow,
A ll he can do is wait for the time to pounce,
L etting all his energy out he

T hen leaps onto his prey,
I ts massive jaw armed with long canine teeth,
G rabbing his prey with his teeth,
E ating his prey and
R oars as loud as he can with pride.

Jamie Cullinane (10)
St Mary's CW Primary School, Brynmawr

The Spotty Animal

Its legs are small and hairy,
Its tail is very furry.
Running through the dark,
Chasing another leopard.

Relaxing on a log,
Suddenly sees a dog,
Then chases the dog.
He catches the dog and cuts him up
Into little pieces, *crunch, crunch, burp!*

Salinder Singh
St Mary's CW Primary School, Brynmawr

The Cheetah

Its coat looks as though it's made from a ray of light.
Its eyes are amber as though they've come from the greatest soil.
Its claws are as sharp as a thousand knives.
Its ears are as strong as though they are as big as the world.
Its spots so black they could get put into space.
Its cubs so furry, they blend in with grass.

Alex Burn (10)
St Mary's CW Primary School, Brynmawr

Ghosts

G hosts are fierce, ghosts are frightening, so run!
H ungry skeletons running around the room, they are scary, so are you! Ha!
O h no! Scary little faces creeping round the room. Oh no! Argh!
S cary skeletons killing people. Oh no!
T angling bones around the room, watch out they will get you. Oh no!

Shane Wilcox
St Mary's CW Primary School, Brynmawr

The Leopard

Spotted feet with hidden sharp claws,
The legs on adults are quite long.
Golden fur dotted with black spots and a golden tail too,
Their eyes are as green as apples,
Their nose is black and they use their teeth
To tear and pierce all their prey.
He is running like a flash of lightning,
He kills the prey,
He will live another day.

Morgan Hinton (10)
St Mary's CW Primary School, Brynmawr

A Pirate Ship

I went on a ship, it was scary,
I looked in a cabin and a ghost jumped out.
I went to hide, then I found some gold,
So I grabbed thousands.
'I will get you,' he said.
Too late.
'Argh!' said the pirate.
I had my pieces of eight.

Kieran Puddle
St Mary's CW Primary School, Brynmawr

Arctic Fox

Their little furry coats blowing in the wind,
Big, bushy tails that drag on the snow,
Little pricky ears that stand up in the breeze,
Black noses twitching and twitching,
Tiny feet with nasty little claws,
What a furry little friend of mine,
I hope he will live on and on.

Ben Morgan Francis-Adams
St Mary's CW Primary School, Brynmawr

Untitled

Paws, baby paws, walking every day,
Using their paws to try to get a hug.

Excellent, loving, marble eyes,
Cute, small, tiny nose.

Perfect little floppy ears,
In a mad race their ears wave.
Every day they want to play around.

Sun sets on the horizon
While the peaceful puppies fall asleep.

Katie Prisk (10)
St Mary's CW Primary School, Brynmawr

Swimming

I like swimming, isn't it fun
To swim in a desert in the warm, warm sun?
I like swimming, isn't it great
To swim in the sea with a really fun mate?
I like swimming, isn't it fab
To bomb in a pool with you best friend's dad?
I like swimming, isn't it a race?
Because when I get older,
I hope I'll have a famous face.

Leah Durham (9)
St Mary's CW Primary School, Brynmawr

Dogs!

D ogs are friendly, they hardly ever bite.
O ld dogs are cute, all they do is lie about.
G o lie down, you little thing.
S ee you in the morning and don't want to hear a thing.

Katie Thompson
St Mary's CW Primary School, Brynmawr

Skeletons

S keletons lurk around,
K illing bugs and looking for you.
E lectricity has been turned off, he will be there!
L ooking for you, run, run . . .
E very time you hear a noise he will be there
T urn around, you see a bone,
O ooooh!
N o, go away!
S pook you out, here I am. 'Argh!'

Lauren Parry (9)
St Mary's CW Primary School, Brynmawr

Kittens

K ittens are cute and cuddly,
I n and out all day.
T he cats in the world are cute,
T he kittens in the world are cute.
E very kitten is cute to me,
N eeding all the love they can get.
S ometimes cats and kittens can be very naughty,
                                  but they're the best.

Taryn Olivia Williams (9)
St Mary's CW Primary School, Brynmawr

My Rabbit

Rabbits are soft and cute,
But mine is the best
Because she is beautiful.
I like her very much.
Her ears are long.
Some rabbits are beautiful,
But my rabbit is lovely.

Luke Collier (8)
St Mary's CW Primary School, Brynmawr

A Holiday

A holiday is fun.
A holiday is nice.
A holiday is being able to play football.
A holiday is going to the beach.
A holiday is going shopping.
A holiday is going in the sea.
A holiday is going in the swimming pool.
A holiday is going to have fun!

Callum Nuth
St Mary's CW Primary School, Brynmawr

An Animal

An animal is a lion that roars loudly.
An animal is a goat that eats you.
An animal can be a zebra that runs with animals.
An animal is a cat that purrs.
An animal is a sort of kitten that is cute.
An animal is a long-necked giraffe.
An animal is a monkey that can swing on trees.
An animal is a kangaroo who leaps away.

Alanna Hill (8)
St Mary's CW Primary School, Brynmawr

Haunted Holidays Are Spooky

Haunted holidays are spooky,
The ghosts frighten you at night.
Every time you come out,
You see a vampire which gives you a fright.
The vampires are spooky,
Scary and horrible.
Witches give you a fright!
Oh no!

Ryan Gardner
St Mary's CW Primary School, Brynmawr

Animals

There are many types of animals
And one that I like
Is to trot on a horse,
On a beautiful site.

There are many types of animals
And another that is nice,
Is a bouncy rabbit,
Which is so nice.

There are many types of animals
And one that is kind
Is a big dog,
Which helps the blind.

Paige Stone (8)
St Mary's CW Primary School, Brynmawr

A Holiday

A holiday is playing football.
A holiday is going on a beach.
A holiday is playing with my friends.
A holiday is having fun.
A holiday is going in a swimming pool.
A holiday is having a sleepover.
A holiday is going shopping.
A holiday is going to the zoo.
I like holidays.

Liam Davies (8)
St Mary's CW Primary School, Brynmawr

My Wish Poem

I would like . . .

A cracker full of kindness,
A bag full of love,
A sack full of happiness,
A bottle full of best friends,
A pot full of welcome,
A plate full of good health.

Louise Bampton
St Mary's CW Primary School, Brynmawr

Bogeys

B ogeys - green, slimy and horrible,
O h no, those things racing down your face,
G ot to go and blow my nose,
E w! You sneezed all over my face.
Y ou love *bogeys!*
S o sorry I sneezed . . .

Joshua Page (9)
St Mary's CW Primary School, Brynmawr

Snow

S nowflakes are ice-blue, some are gold, some are even white.
N oses go bright red in the snow, arms and legs, bright white.
O range sun is setting in the sky, the snow is melting, it's time
                                            to say goodbye.
W hen we go in, we have to take the warm clothes off and sit
                                            by the fire.

Chloe Williams (10)
St Mary's CW Primary School, Brynmawr